Raising and Praising Girls

Elizabeth Hartley Brewer

Vermilion
LONDON

5 7 9 10 8 6

First published in the United Kingdom in 2005 by Vermilion,
an imprint of Ebury Publishing
Random House UK Ltd
Random House, 20 Vauxhall Bridge Road, London SW1V 2SA

www.randomhouse.co.uk

Addresses for companies within
The Random House Group Limited can be found at:
www.randomhouse.co.uk/offices.htm

The Random House Group Limited Reg. No. 954009

A CIP catalogue record for this book
is available from the British Library

ISBN 9780091906733

The Random House Group Limited supports the Forest Stewardship
Council® (FSC®), the leading international forest certification organisation.
All our titles that are printed on Greenpeace approved FSC® certified paper
carry the FSC® logo. Our paper procurement policy can be found at
www.randomhouse.co.uk/environment

Printed and bound in Great Britain by
CPI Antony Rowe, Chippenham, Wiltshire

Contents

	Introduction	1
1	Understanding Praise, and How Girls React to it	5
2	The Purpose of Praise	9
3	Keeping Praise Effective: Ten basic principles	32
4	Ages and Stages: Adapting to development	54
5	What to Notice and Encourage: Being creative	78
6	The Language of Praise: Ways to say it, and do it	100
7	Common Mistakes to Try to Avoid	122
8	Bribes, Rewards and Incentives	144
9	Using Praise to Encourage Learning and Behaviour	166
10	Avoiding the Perils of Perfectionism	190
11	Praise and You	212
	Postscript	234

For Lynette, Rosemary, Rosalind and Hugh.
And with grateful thanks to all the young people and
adults who shared their stories with me.

Introduction

This book has been written for parents with girls of any age – babies, toddlers and teenagers – and for teachers. Most of the tips cover general principles but several are age-specific and show how our praise style should change as our girls grow. One of the most important lessons we have learnt over the last two to three decades is how much all children benefit from receiving praise from parents and teachers. Children respond far better to positive feedback and encouragement than they do to threats, criticism and punishment. Many parents and teachers found it hard to use what they felt to be fulsome words; and although some still do, most people are now sufficiently familiar and comfortable with the phrases commonly used to hand out praise in good measure.

Praise has been viewed as the way to boost children's self-esteem, to help them feel confident and to fulfil their potential and be at ease with themselves. Many won't realise that using praise also has wider benefits for individual children and society, because it can help to encourage self-discipline and moral behaviour. However, nothing about parenting or children is straightforward. Girls and boys, for example, often react to praise in different ways and need their confidence reinforced in different areas. We are also beginning to realise that if praise is over-used, used for particular personal motives or directed at the wrong kind of activity, it may actually be unhelpful. When praise is over-used, over-hyped or belies the truth, girls may either become praise dependent and require constant affirmation and approval, or become indifferent to it. Another possibility is that they may start to mistrust either the message or the messenger, wasting everyone's breath; or they might come to think they're super-clever and special and annoy people with their self-importance, when in truth they're simply normal. Any child can also feel suffocated by a continuous positive or negative commentary on her every move; and may behave outrageously to shake off the microscopic attention and constant judgement.

In addition, there is growing concern that over-exposure to praise has led to children being ruined by rewards, dulled by 'dumbing down' and incapacitated by anxiety or, at the very least, easily wrong-footed when faced with real challenges. For praise to be reliably effective, we have to be careful, subtle and understand fully its pros and cons, wider value and the approaches that are safest given girls' particular sensitivities.

This is what this book sets out to achieve. The early chapters (1–6) present the basic principles, tactics and purposes of praise. Chapter One develops an understanding of praise that underpins the thinking behind the 100 tips that are spread equally between the remaining ten chapters. Chapter Four enables readers to reflect upon important features of child development, and so relate the principles and tactics to the age and developmental stage of any girl. The later chapters (7–10) consider the subtleties and potential dangers of praise, and the final one invites readers to self-reflect. Each tip has been written to stand alone and so can be dipped into at random, but readers may benefit initially from reading consecutively, at least the introduction to each chapter, to gain a sense of the direction and argument. It is a book to revisit on many occasions.

To offer a flavour of what this book will help you to understand, consider the following questions and try to spot the key differences between the possible responses:

When your daughter does particularly well, which might you say?
* I'm really proud of you for managing that!
* I hope you feel proud of yourself – you should.
* You probably feel really proud to have achieved that.
* I feel so proud of you and proud that you're my child.

If your daughter gets into the school swimming team, would you . . .?
* Say, Great! How many others tried for how many places?
* Promise to continue the trips to the pool to develop her skills further.
* Go as a family to every match to give her support.
* Attend yourself and shout encouragement from the side.

When your daughter tidies her room without being told, would you . . .?

- Give her a hug and bring her a hot or cold drink.
- Say thanks, but laugh and say you wonder how long it will last.
- Give her money, and hope this will persuade her to carry on the good work.
- Comment favourably on the improvement and ask what triggered the idea.

. . . Now read on!

CHAPTER 1

Understanding Praise, and How Girls React to it

Children love praise; of course they do, for most of us thrive on compliments and appreciation. Despite the pleasure it gives, children should be praised for more than just the delight it brings them or that it helps them try harder. Praise needs to be a central part of raising children because it meets most of their fundamental needs. In other words, praise is not merely a bit of luxury, some additional fancy wrapping that we can leave off if we prefer. Children need to feel important and significant to someone, to believe that someone cares enough to cherish them, and this is at least as important as being properly fed and clothed. Children need to feel secure and trust and rely on that care, which they can when they feel valued and central to their carer's life. They also need friendly and warm guidance, support and direction about how they should lead their lives through to adolescence, so they need to hear what it is they should do rather than how they constantly fall short and disappoint. And in order for a girl to flourish, she needs to know and be told she is capable, is enjoyed and gives pleasure – particularly to her parents.

Praise tends to be thought of as something spoken, put into words, but we can convey our pleasure, approval and appreciation in many ways. Hugs, smiles, rewards and touches, as we see in Chapter Six, all have their part to play and can sometimes be more effective because they can be more spontaneous and more direct. Even the spoken vocabulary of praise is more varied than at first appears, for the term 'praise' includes many types of phrase and expression that convey appreciation, acknowledgement or pure delight. The differences are important, as will become clear as the tips are explored.

It is deeply frustrating to realise that not all praise is helpful: just when we thought we were getting it right, people are saying we could be getting it wrong. The good news is that it is not complicated to work out which styles and phrases are likely to support achievement and which sentiments can become confusing or burdensome and could cause our children difficulty. Effective relationships are always those that manage to keep a range of needs, styles and objectives in balance. The essence of constructive praise is that it is useful and encouraging: it provides relevant detailed information; it is believable so it is neither hollow nor false; and it may also show the way forward. Most important, the recipient should remain in full charge of her progress and be given opportunities to become confident in her ability to judge things for herself.

The energy that enables girls to take advantage of opportunity is self-belief. Self-belief is fuelled when girls feel genuinely capable because they know in detail what it was they did right (which means they know they can do it again), because they have acknowledged the mistakes they made in the past and now know how to avoid them (which means failures have been faced, not ignored) and because they feel certain that they are unconditionally loved and accepted for who they are, not for matching up to someone else's ideal or for something they're especially good at. It is rarely helpful to celebrate every success and ignore every failure, for just as certain types of praise can be unhelpful, criticism can be constructive – when mistakes are acknowledged, identified and ironed out girls learn from them.

Girls tend to be more conformist than boys and like to tow the line and receive approval. Most enjoy being 'good', to the extent that girls are the goody goodies and are far more likely to strive to be teacher's pet. Few boys are ever described as a goody goody. But the danger is that girls have a propensity to do things not because they judge it to be right or helpful but in order to get into or stay in other people's good books. They are therefore far more prey to flattery than boys, more likely to mould themselves on key individuals' expectations and can become cut off from their true selves, which means that they may have fewer opportunities to establish a clear personal identity.

With girls, it is important not to over-emphasise 'good' behaviour. Obedience, diligence, cleanliness and tidiness are certainly easier for parents to live with, but far more than this is required if a child is to become a successful adult. Eating disorder specialists comment frequently on female sufferers' perfectionism, their regular handwriting, their impressive personal organisation, their sensitivity, high standards and achievements and desire to please. Yet this success often masks a deeper discontent and doubt directed at the self. What girls need in today's competitive world is the ability to stand up for themselves, to explore, be creative and to take risks, which raises the likelihood of mistakes and mess. Praise needs to boost a girl's inner confidence – her underlying capability and her capacity to judge for herself – rather than highlight effort and outcomes that have been defined as desirable by someone else. When girls become 'clones' and model themselves on an idealised image to get approval, it can mean that they fear failure.

Girls enjoy pleasing adults and respect success in others, so they remain happy to receive praise publicly. Achievements may encourage others to greater effort but some may become bitchy to offset the envy they feel. Nonetheless, those who do well often remain convinced it was a fluke, not due to their talent. They need to be given details about what they did right and told that it is absolutely okay to make mistakes and fail sometimes.

CHAPTER 2

The Purpose of Praise

What is praise for? It may seem an unnecessary question to ask but it is important to be clear about what it is we are trying to achieve to help us check whether what we say and do is all-round beneficial with no negative side effects. For example, parents of course want to help their daughters grow up with good self-esteem to confound the age-old assumption that women do not or cannot make it to the top. Self-esteem and strong self-belief are, indeed, valuable attributes. Nonetheless, their value is undermined if they come at the expense of sound self-knowledge (because they are told they're wonderful at everything), sound friendships (because friends are put off by the resulting interfering bossiness) and determination and perseverance because girls are always shielded from challenges and setbacks. Praising certain reactions and behaviour, such as thoughtfulness, can help to develop moral awareness, and children can be encouraged to notice their effect on other people. But if piling on praise leads to self-obsession and over-confidence, a girl's awareness of her impact on other people could be dulled. In order to decide whether our affirmative comments and actions are overall helpful, we should acknowledge the full range of possible desirable goals and the different categories and styles of positive feedback.

Here are some terms, all of which begin with the letter A, that help us to focus on the varied, deeper purposes of praise beyond the obvious ones.

Affirm; Appreciate; Approve; Admire; Attend; Anticipate;
Achieve; Acknowledge; be Aware and Alert; Aspiration

Each of these ten simple objectives is explored as a separate tip in this chapter.

It is useful to consider praise in terms of time zones. Although each encounter and incident is in the present, a key purpose of praise – and of support and encouragement – is to help our daughters or the girls in our charge feel optimistic about their future, comfortable with the route they have travelled from the past, as well as content with the present. When we *encourage* them, our focus is on the future – we try to convince any girl she will overcome any current difficulty to be successful thereafter. We therefore generate faith, hope and confidence and give her heart. When we clearly *enjoy* her company and achievements, we indicate our happiness and pleasure with who she is, in the present. When we *endorse* her actions, her view of the world, her approaches to learning and her feelings, we are accepting those bits of her that have been fashioned by her past.

If girls are comfortable about their past behaviour and experiences, even if these were difficult, they are better able to look optimistically at the future. It is not helpful for parents or significant others to make a girl feel either ashamed of or guilty about her past or to wipe it out in any attempt to refocus and start again.

1 Affirm – to help her feel strong

Q: If parents don't praise you directly, how else might you know that they're pleased with you?

A: You can tell by their face, which shows they're proud. (8)

A: When she smiles at you, you kind of know. It makes me feel proud of myself. (9)

To affirm a child is to make a clear statement that confirms and accepts her as she is. The word has its origins in a Latin word that means 'strong'. It therefore implies strength. When we affirm a child, we offer a firm statement of strong support, but it also gives children strength when they hear it.

To affirm is to make a neutral, judgement-free statement. Its essence is descriptive. An affirmation is powerful and valuable because it is able to encompass the past, present and future – to endorse and encourage. We do not have to wait for any particular event or achievement to speak out. We can help our daughter to understand who she is at any time by describing what we see – her qualities and personality, likes and dislikes, particular talents – and then confirm how much we enjoy and love her as she is.

Parents

* think of ways to describe how she thinks and does things that will 'firm her up', make her feel confident and strong inside:
– 'I love the way your eyes crinkle at the edges when you laugh'
– 'I've noticed how well you organised everyone to . . ., which makes me think you're responsible enough to go into town with friends at the weekend'

* Ask her to help you with tasks either because she is good company or because she's good at that sort of thing

Teachers

* 'I like your ideas and what you are trying to say. They'd be clearer and more powerful if you separated them out. Try writing each idea down and thinking how they link to the rest'

* 'of course you will feel cross that Carl is using the computer before you, but alphabetical order is what the class agreed'

2 Appreciate her achievements

You need to believe you can do it. (10)

For a young child, every day brings fresh challenges and fresh achievements. One day she can't do something, yet the next she can. Life is a growing experience in which each day more becomes manageable so competence can blossom. These achievements become the expression of being and it is essential that they are fully appreciated.

One of the meanings of 'appreciate' is, be sensitive to. That is a significant definition. It suggests we should be sufficiently sensitive to see things on her level and in her terms: in relation to her challenges and difficulties, her limitations and capabilities, not our expectations.

'Appreciation' also covers the notion of value increasing, as in the value of houses or other forms of saving. Each child can be viewed as our most valuable asset. She will see that she goes up in your estimation each time you appreciate her and what she has managed to achieve. Of course you love her too, and she remains as important to you as ever, but every child really flies if she feels that those on whom she relies and whom she loves to the bottom of her being believe she has the potential to develop and impress.

Parents

* 'achievement' can be very widely interpreted: any advance in reading level, sociability, maths, height and reach, ball skills, being able to dress unaided, confidence, learning to swim, pack bags for school or an overnight with a friend, can be openly appreciated

* appreciation energises – when girls hear your appreciation they feel able to move forward. Those who receive little can get emotionally and developmentally stuck and become demoralised

Teachers

* many schools have reward systems that acknowledge achievement for each individual, rather than what is exceptional for the group

* appreciate a wide variety of skills and knowledge, not simply those related to academic learning on which most lessons concentrate

* appreciate, in other words be sensitive to, each child's vulnerabilities. Some may need to hear it more frequently

3 Approve of who she is

When I get praise, it makes me feel special. (8)

Approval is the green light to grow, to carry on in the same way because she is good and lovely and fine as she is. Girls need this not only from their mothers, but also – as they enter their pre-teens – from their fathers if this is feasible. As soon as girls start to fashion their individual identity around being female, from about the age of eight, they benefit from having a mature male who will not just approve of her but also show profound respect for her as she explores ideas of gender differences, different styles of relationship with the opposite sex she might expect and what being female might mean for her. Male friends, uncles or cousins or a friendly neighbour may be able to step in where a father is not available. In any case, mothers should be careful not to disparage men in general because girls need to be able to explore relationships with the opposite sex confidently.

But gender is only one aspect of her identity – one of the later spoonfuls of colour added to her personality palette. She is already an individual and she needs to feel approved of for all her strengths, weaknesses, fears, habits and eccentricities.

Parents

* hear her side of the story – assume the best of her, not the worst

* let her tell you about her disappointments and realise what they mean to her

* respect her ideas – of what to play or wear; her methods – how to study; and her preferences when these are important

* listen to what she has to say, keeping your opinions to yourself unless she asks for them

Teachers

* avoid stereotyping – each girl is an individual, not a replica of anyone, even an older sibling

* acknowledge that each student's point of view will be the result of her unique experiences over the years

* accept that different children learn in different ways and be tolerant of each one's preferred style

4 Admire rather than adore

When parents put their daughters on a pedestal, it presents them with a very hard act to follow. Most of them would prefer not to have that pressure. The following conversation between a mother and her two-year-old daughter highlights the problem. 'I adore you, Susie!' 'Don't adore me, mummy.' 'Why not?' 'Because I cry too much.'

What Susie was trying to say was: It is too much for me always to behave in a way that pleases you and makes you adore me. I know I'm not that good all the time, because I cry a lot which makes you cross and I can tell that you don't adore me then.

Adoration is a form of worship and children don't want to be treated as a god. We may feel it privately, for most of us think our children are from heaven, but we should express something more measured. We can admire how any girl in our care copes in a particular situation; admire how she manages to overcome her fears or admire how she approaches a problem. She will realise she is in command during these moments and the occasion is specific. What she certainly cannot directly control are our feelings: these are our business and it is unfair to load her with any responsibility for these. Even when she cries we should show we love her for being who she is.

Parents

* don't put her on a pedestal. Let her feel special to you because she is yours, but let her feel normal in relation to her peers

* show admiration for what she does: 'Well spotted', 'Nice work!', 'Brilliant idea', but don't worship the ground she walks on

* keep her free of emotional obligations to you: don't require her to earn your love or behave in order to keep you entranced

Teachers

* teachers are unlikely to 'adore' a particular child in their class, but having one or two favourites is quite common. Girls who are vulnerable may interpret not being a favourite as being actually out of favour, which may undermine their willingness to work well with you

* try to keep even your admiration in proportion and always keep it private; at the very least, find some facet in every student that you can respect and admire

5 Attention is what all girls really want

I hate it when adults ignore me! It makes me feel like an ant. (10)

Children need to be noticed. They are very small creatures in a very big world which is sure to appear huge, confusing and even intimidating to them. Our supportive attention fires them up; it gives them the energy and confidence to find their way. Without it, they can feel lost and as small and insignificant as an ant.

Girls need appreciative attention. When children are young, they are learning at a speed that would exhaust most adults. What gives them special pleasure is to gain greater control of their life and more independence as they become taller, stronger, more dextrous and better coordinated. They can acquire an enormous sense of pride in their achievements as they reach the top of the climbing frame, learn to jump in the deep end of the swimming pool, skip with ropes or simply become sufficiently tall to open the freezer or reach the tap or light switch. At these moments of personal triumph, their whole self shouts 'look at me!' If we are absent either physically or mentally, they could become dejected and crestfallen.

Parents

* remember that attention-seeking is usually attention-needing. Give her more attention if she starts to pester and irritate, but only once she has calmed down

* when you are with her, give her your full attention: don't answer the telephone; don't sneak in a coffee with a friend on your special trip out; and refer to any special chats or episodes later, so she knows you logged them

* think of the everyday things you do that she might feel excluded from and ways she could become more involved; she's bound to want to see where you work, for example

Teachers

* girls who don't demand attention are easy to take for granted. They could be simply being 'good', having no troubles lurking underneath. But troubled girls often become quiet, and may need sensitive attention

* identify the girls you have contact with who are quiet or withdrawn or who have 'gone off the boil'. Speak briefly to each of them around school over the next three to four weeks or just smile and say, 'How's things?'

* if a quiet girl is with friends when you pass, either leave it or include a practical issue as well as something affirming. She'll then have an easier answer for friends if they query her

6 Anticipate her problems and feelings

Girls are inclined to be natural worriers, so much so that they can sometimes seem to take on the cares of the world – especially during their early teens when their moral senses reach maturity. They will worry about any difficulties their mum might be experiencing, their pet's illnesses or about problems that their close friends have shared with them. They are also far more likely than boys to think ahead and become concerned about any forthcoming pressures or changes to their life. Parents can help a great deal if they take a moment to try to anticipate their daughter's likely feelings and reactions and reduce the anxiety.

Demonstrate by example and try to anticipate how she may respond to something potentially difficult that is coming up in order to help her prepare. Encourage her to be honest about and reflect on her feelings by chatting about how you felt when it happened to you, or say, 'I imagine that was difficult for you.' Although we would not want to generate anxiety where none existed, a girl can be relieved to discover someone understands their worry, especially if she has tried to disguise it.

Parents

* anticipate how she might react to something that is about to happen. If she might be distressed or disappointed, tell her you realise this and address the details that may worry her to put her more at ease. She will at least feel accepted and understood

* through positive feedback and prompting, lots of talk that focuses on today's, yesterday's and tomorrow's events, we can help to allay her fears and prepare for other people's likely reactions

* rather than allow her to stay locked safely in the present, help her to reflect on the past and future and make sense of these if they are uncomfortable

Teachers

* try to imagine the particular difficulty a girl who is struggling might confront with a particular assignment. Approach her and acknowledge this, perhaps suggesting a few helpful guidelines

* give her faith in her ability to complete the task well enough in a way that represents a learning advance for her

7 Help her achieve her aims

Aged 9, my daughter decided she wanted to redecorate the dolls' house her uncle had made her. She wanted to stick fresh wallpaper in every room, put new carpets down, hang new curtains and repaint the front. It was a big project that she could not manage without help to acquire usable scraps of material (that were to colour coordinate) and to cut pieces to size. She was determined to complete the project, and did so, with lots of parental input. The valuable lessons she learnt were that it is safe to have aims, how to realise and complete a project, how she could rely on us to help her out.

Girls can be dogged and determined: their perseverance is generally better than that of boys of a similar age. Their weakness is that sometimes they need to have everything perfect. They can get angry and frustrated and discard the offending item or piece of work because the inevitable flaws are unacceptable. They should be assured that, from time to time, good enough often works well enough so she should adjust her standards.

Parents

* whereas it may be pushy to ensure girls reach the goals we determine, it is wholly supportive and encouraging when we help her identify practical pathways to those she sets for herself

* help her to set out a detailed plan that will enable her to achieve her more challenging aspirations

* ask her what equipment or help she needs, but don't take over and make it your project

Teachers

* it is important that children receive constructive feedback that helps them to learn, develop their understanding and, through this process, learn how increasingly to manage their own progress

* girls will be helped to achieve their aims, and manage without constant confirmation that they're doing fine, when they plan their own work, then carry out their plan, ending with a review of what went right and wrong in order to assess how to approach that same task next time. This is known as 'feedback for learning'; in shorthand, plan, do, review, then reframe the task

8 Acknowledge her personal strengths

Girls don't have to be 'good at' something before they gain our attention and regard. Each will possess personal qualities, inclinations, interests and strengths that can be noted, appreciated and – most importantly – brought to her attention. Praise should always encompass far more than pats on the back for specific accomplishments. Sometimes, an aggressive determination will be her route to achievement, and that style of working should be accepted if that is her way.

If we reflect back and give a name to some of the warmer qualities she demonstrates to us or friends, as well as to those strengths such as perseverance or determination that encourage achievement, she will be able to develop a picture of her whole self just as she sees her whole physical self in a mirror. It will help her to value all her qualities, not just her schoolwork.

The kinds of personal strengths we can acknowledge and encourage in our daughters include thoughtfulness, understanding, good at sharing, caring, forthrightness, curiosity, sense of humour, good memory, well-organised, imaginative, able to relax, carefree, good powers of concentration, interested in ideas and well-coordinated.

Parents

* acknowledge the full range of her possible talents and interests

* acknowledge positive thoughts as well as positive deeds

* focus on the necessary 'doing' aspects of achievement – the inclination to try – as well as the amount she tried by the end of the process

Teachers

* acknowledge that each child is an individual with rights to be heard and respected

* list the personal strengths of any girl whose behaviour is causing concern and make sure she and other children realise you appreciate these

* choose her to perform any task that might develop or demonstrate her personal strengths

* take care to balance out your attention sufficiently so an attempt to help one individual does not appear as favouritism

9 Be aware and alert

We cannot talk about what we have noticed unless we remain aware of her moods, what has delighted her, her preferences and so on. We can be with our child all day without really noticing any of these, or we can see our daughter for only two or three hours a day and be acutely sensitive to her body language, expressions, tone of voice, choices and demeanour.

Being aware does not necessarily mean we should discuss every concern or interpretation then and there but we would be wise to note it and watch for a possible pattern: too much expressed 'sensitivity' can feel intrusive. 'Stop trying to get inside my head!' was the frustrated cry of one eleven-year-old to her mother when she was trying hard to be empathic. Especially after a tiring day at school, children want to relax, remain quiet and reflect. Any rebuff, often indicated by a curt 'fine', is not necessarily a sign of big trouble she'd rather keep private, just the need to be quiet and alone for a while.

Parents

* watch discreetly how she relates to her brothers and sisters; compliment her if she is able to manage any disputes, holds her own without aggression or if she ignores being baited by others

* make a mental note of which events enthuse her and which tend to make her sad or disappointed

* be careful not to seem like a spy: 'I have generally noticed / been aware / it's become clear to me that . . .' is better than, 'I have been watching you from a distance and I've seen you be really . . .'

* if something important is to happen at school – a test, a notable visitor, a special fun class, a class play – ensure you remember to ask how it went

Teachers

* it is easy to comment positively on students' work when they hand it in as an assignment but less easy to remark on their wider attitudes and supportive behaviour unless you look out for these

* be alert for signs of sadness or depression; a sensitivity to these will imply you have bothered to notice and know her well enough to realise things aren't quite right

10 Her, not your, aspirations matter most

I've already decided. She's going to be a doctor when she grows up. I've set my heart on it and I'm going to do everything I can to get her interested in human biology and how the body works as she goes through school!

This single mum had had a hard time and was desperate to give her daughter a better life. She thought that giving her clear aspirations for a stable and successful professional future would be the best she could do for her. Her daughter is still too young to know whether she will get her way! While it is certainly better that we look hopefully on her future prospects than professing doubt and derision, it is, though, potentially dangerous to be as pre-determined as this mum.

She may, for example, stifle some special interest that develops for fear it could divert events from her chosen path. Her dreams may become obvious and her daughter may be tempted to thwart her from spite. Her daughter may, though, enjoy following this destiny and see it as a gently amusing game. The most valuable thing we can nurture in our daughter is the confidence, optimism, trust, motivation, space and self-determination that she may develop her own aspirations.

Parents

* offer plenty of attention, affirmation and structure so she has the confidence to imagine herself doing well and the creativity to aspire

* help to ground those aspirations in reality by discussing practical plans for making them happen

* even small girls will express wishes and desires: 'I want to draw a plan of the back garden', 'I'd like to play a hospital game when Cara comes over', 'I'd like to play the guitar'. If you help to make these happen, she will know it is safe to dream and possible to influence her destiny

* help to make her future feel safe and full of potential by creating a secure present

Teachers

* learning should help us all to explore 'our possible selves' – it should open up possibilities not close them down

* help girls to express their aspirations and narrow down the possible routes to achieving them. After a good piece of work, or a good term, ask where she sees this leading because you see all doors opening for her

* from a young age girls can be encouraged to think ahead and conceive of what they might do or be as an adult, where they might live or what their favoured pastimes will be. The future should offer potential, not be avoided and remain empty

CHAPTER 3

Keeping Praise Effective: Ten basic principles

Keeping praise effective is important. There is no point praising a girl if she is going to end up feeling oppressed or manipulated by it, or resentful because we have not got it right. Resentful children have a tendency to hit back where it hurts most, so if we show that her performance in netball or swimming tournaments, in school or on the stage is the part of her that really matters to us, that could be what she decides to opt out of either to pay us back for our interference or to deflect the constant pressure.

We praise children because we believe it helps them, so there is no point, either, in trying to build a child's confidence if it leads to the opposite: a child with an unstable sense of self-worth who needs regular reinforcement and frequent success to remain convinced of her ability and our approval. It is not good when any child becomes so used to praise that its absence can be interpreted as disapproval or disappointment. It seems a tricky path to tread, but it is not so difficult if the ten basic principles of constructive praise, set out in the next ten tips, are followed.

The hallmarks of constructive praise are that it should:

- *strengthen self-belief*, so it should generalise the achievement where possible and pay as much attention to a girl's capacity to achieve as to the quality of any specific outcome, as well as be believable. Possible comments are, 'You're good at *that sort of thing*' or, 'Now you've done it once, that should give you the confidence to understand it next time and thereafter.'
- *highlight the way forward*, so is useful
- *leave her with the possibility and opportunity to change*, be different or to do something differently next time. It should not, therefore, lock any girl into a single way to please, perform or do things by being too narrow and focused. Children develop and change as they mature and grow, as adults do, which is one of the potential delights of living for all of us.
- *avoid dependency*, by encouraging her gradually to judge things for herself, by making clear your confidence in her ability to do so and by leaving her in charge of her development. It will also help her to realise that what matters most is the pattern of her personal progress and learning, not the precise outcome on any specific occasion.

11 Let her impress you

Girls love it when someone they respect and admire shows clearly and freely they are genuinely impressed by something they have done. Showing and stating you are impressed is a very effective and straightforward form of praise, which helps a girl to stand more upright, inspired by extra confidence and pleasure.

Being impressed sidesteps the judgement that is implied in so much praise. Most important, it is unconditional. 'I am really impressed!' or 'That was impressive!' says it all – no ifs and buts to qualify or detract from the message. There is nothing grudging about being impressed and when girls hear it they are able to feel appreciated and more confident.

Mothers and fathers who are able to be impressed with their daughter clear the air of competition. It levels the playing field, for it shows you don't need to prove that you are stronger, better and more clever. And being impressed doesn't mean a girl has got the better of you in some way or will stop trying. It simply signifies respect and admiration, which is what girls, like boys, thirst for.

Parents

* compare her favourably with you as a child: 'I couldn't have managed that when I was your age', 'I wish I'd been able to do that/draw/sing as well as you can'

* 'I thought you played impressively well. Were you pleased with what you did?'

* when playing any game, let a small child win in little ways, and show you're impressed with her increasing skill

* ask her to help you fix things, organise things, decide things, clean things then say, 'You're ace at that. You were really useful'

Teachers

* 'you showed an impressive degree of understanding in that essay'

* 'I'm impressed that this piece of work was so much better laid out. It must have taken you longer, but thanks for giving it extra time. It was worth it'

* 'that's an impressive improvement. Well done!'

* give quieter girls responsibilities, such as reporting back on group discussions and looking up information for everyone's benefit. Show how impressed you are with the outcome

12 Make it mean something – be specific

I prefer praise from my mum. She explains why it's good or bad, which is better. (8)

It helps self-doubting girls to trust their ability if praise is descriptive and specific: related to a particular piece of work, achievement or action. Describing something in detail proves without doubt you have noticed your daughter's effort or thoughtfulness, but your observations also help the feedback to be accurate, relevant and persuasive while having the additional advantage of being non-judgemental.

It is very common for girls to focus on their mistakes rather than their achievements. While it is important that girls don't shy away from shortcomings, adults must be careful not to say things in a manner that feeds any nascent self-doubt. Girls must be clearly told the root of their successes to realise it was not fluke or the result of easy questions on the day, so that it strengthens her self-belief. Similarly, any disappointing results should be analysed with specific reference to techniques, knowledge gaps and so on, rather then personal weakness. This will both help her to see the way to improve and boost her confidence for next time because she can then understand what it is she's doing right and will know she can repeat it.

Parents

* describe in some detail what she's done that is pleasing so she's clear what's right about her approach and what she needs to repeat next time

* when looking at her picture or painting, discuss the colours used or the size or shape. Ask why or whether she likes what she's done, whether she planned it or if it just turned out that way

* describe what you appreciated about how she behaved after an event rather than comment every few minutes as the occasion unfolds

Teachers

* encourage girls to evaluate each other's work, not to encourage competition but so they may learn from each other, be less secretive and be more descriptive and less triumphal about what counts as quality

* girls need to know in detail what they did right and wrong so comments and marks should be full and clear at the same time as encouraging

* help her to feel it is okay to be proud of good enough work. 'I bet you felt pretty happy with this piece of work. You should have done'

13 Keep praise private

You don't like it when they show it off to other people, then everyone looks at you. It's so embarrassing. It's something that should be kept between the parent and child, though I don't mind if my sister knows – she's much older. Sometimes they say it to other parents who say their child did well, too, when you know they didn't! It's more mums than dads. They gossip. (10)

Girls are happier than boys to receive formal praise at school. Perhaps they are more inclined to strive in order to impress others, so they like others to know when they succeed. The girls in one single sex school complained that special achievements, for example in local sporting, academic or drama competitions, were no longer getting a mention in the school newsletter, and they asked for this to be changed. The desire for public accolade should, though, be limited where possible, because it encourages a dangerous focus on striving for public status instead of a healthier interest in self-development.

At home, praise and criticism should be a private matter between parent and daughter, not paraded regularly to others or as something for any siblings to exploit or resent. Bigger achievements may, of course, be openly celebrated – though you should first check she is happy with this plan.

Parents

* celebration is a public statement, but everyday praise and encouragement should be private

* ask yourself whose business this is. Usually, it relates only to parent and child, for it is no one else's responsibility

* keeping praise private helps to keep it in proportion. The more people you tell, or the more people present when you say it to her, the more it will seem to grow in importance and court unintended consequences

Teachers

* private praise encourages a safer focus on her personal progress. Public praise may encourage unhelpful competition, tempting girls to work for the wrong reasons

* if you profile someone's achievement in, for example, an assembly, check afterwards whether she was comfortable with the experience

* don't forget the parents. Some girls might prefer to have a note sent home rather than their classmates knowing of an accomplishment

* have a quiet word with a pupil as she leaves the class if you want to say a special well done

14 Let her take all the credit

It is often taken as a sign of good teaching or parenting if a child excels, so either adult may seek to claim credit when a daughter, pupil or class does well. Of course we might have had some influence, by reading to her a great deal when she was young, driving her to and from extra classes or training, helping her with her maths when stuck, encouraging her to keep a daily diary on special holidays or nurturing any special fascination with botany, astronomy or breeds of dog that might have livened her mind. But her actual achievement – on the day – is always hers and it is cruel, selfish and short-sighted to suggest anything else. If we need to boost our own self-esteem through claiming success on the back of our child's, the most obvious message is that success is something she, too, needs before she can feel acceptable and complete.

In the same vein, if we help in a manner that makes her believe – or means she cannot be sure – that her success was down to her own efforts only, it dilutes the potential gain in self-belief and confidence, which would be a great pity if she could, indeed, have achieved it on her own.

Parents

* never attribute any of her success to you. Make it clear that she can feel one hundred per cent it was her work; otherwise, she may feel she needs you next time too

* if you find yourself saying, 'That homework we did . . . What was our mark?', realise that you could be about to walk off not only with some of the credit but also with ownership of the work!

* if she refers to your help, restate it was she who delivered on the day, and further help won't be necessary

Teachers

* in the context of league tables, it is hard not to claim much of the credit if a whole class does better than expected. Nevertheless, each student must feel she did it herself, even if she was well-taught by you!

* the more detail a girl has about why she did well, the more she can see and believe it was her knowledge, learning and application that took her there

15 Be careful with judgement

My friend was very keen on manners. Her little girl had to be polite and aware of others at all times, even though she was only five or six. She was praised well for this. But if she bumped into someone while walking down the street, dropped a sweet wrapper or didn't think to step aside for a pushchair, she was reprimanded for her disappointing behaviour. She couldn't cope with being judged for things she was too young to control and at home she regressed, behaving like a baby.

Children need to be noticed rather than judged. It is fine to evaluate some of what they do but it is not fine to be judgemental about who they are. When children are young they cannot conceptualise this distinction, so they take all criticism personally and conclude they are in some way bad. They don't want to be evaluated from dawn to dusk, being monitored constantly and required to stay in line. If this happens, girls can develop 'learned helplessness', where they demand so much help it removes the risk of getting anything wrong. Children thrive when they are open and feel free within safe limits, not where they are constantly looking out for the carrot, reward or stick.

Parents

* ensure your expectations are age appropriate. Young girls cannot help being careless

* keep shame and guilt out of it, until she is about ten years old when she has the capacity to control and self monitor and can clearly separate what she does from who she is

* you bring about what you fear. Girls will flaunt bad behaviour if they are told off continually. It ends the waiting and puts them in control so is less humiliating

* expectations must always be appropriate and criticism reserved for actions that girls can easily change

Teachers

* encourage girls to assess their own work

* keep feedback neutral and descriptive rather than either fulsome or harsh and negative

* shame often encourages girls to ignore or reject suggestions for improvement, use it very sparingly

16 Be truthful, not gushing

It can get annoying if it's said over and over again. Sometimes it's for something really small, like getting ten simple sums right, and my mum goes on and on about it. (8)

Even young girls can detect what they might view as 'gush and mush' – over-enthusiastic adulation that seems unrelated to the effort that was entailed and was certainly not expected, let alone desired. It is too emotional, too intimate and may feel especially inappropriate if a girl achieved something entirely to satisfy herself. Gushing praise also encourages a girl to believe that she is responsible for a parent's excessive delight, and that it is the parent's delight that counts. What counts, of course, is her own sense of pride, fulfilment and pleasure – she must eventually do things to a standard to please herself, not to gain riotous applause from the parental gallery.

False praise is not only offensive and insulting; it also does not help any child or young person to develop good judgement. Over time, she must learn to judge her effort and work herself. If we go overboard when she knows something could have been done better, she will find it harder to tell what is good enough and what could be improved upon. For any girl who tends to over-value her work, gushing will be particularly unhelpful.

Parents

* don't pretend, but be positive and upbeat where you can. Make the scope for improvement very clear and encourage her to accept and understand shortcomings. 'I don't quite call this a tidied room. You've done well so far but that pile of magazines still needs sorting. When you've finished, I'll bring you up a drink and admire the room!'

* focus on the pleasure she gets, so she learns to perform for her benefit, not yours

Teachers

* some children need more of a boost and find measured praise hard to believe. However, these girls just need praise more often, not more enthusiastically or exaggeratedly, because they won't believe that either

* if you are honest but encouraging about the bad, students will be more inclined to believe honestly-given praise

17 Praise the process not the product

Many sceptics of the value of praise complain that the quality of the product does matter, and more than the process. What is the point, they argue, in claiming something is good when it is not, and in ignoring the reason – that someone simply did not try hard enough when they could obviously do better?

Naturally, at some point quality does matter and girls should, indeed, be called to account if they failed to make any effort. But trying is always valuable – no one makes any progress without some commitment and effort applied to learning more or doing better. At the beginning of any new challenge, effort is necessarily often crude and inefficient and the product flawed compared with what we could do, but that is how we all started and we have survived! Children cannot continuously be told something is not good enough. Effort involves skills such as determination and tenacity and these need to be valued and encouraged.

Parents

* remember that 'process' includes interest, effort, determination and good work habits, and these characteristics should all be valued as part of learning and growing

* take any effort mark supplied by your daughter's school seriously. Sensitive to her age and stage, schools often judge effort better than parents

* young children don't understand what it means to concentrate. Encourage this by reading longer stories to her or playing board games that take time, patience and thought

* learning is an emotional activity, so ask if it was hard, if she worried about the outcome or if she faltered in the middle

Teachers

* through use of the 'plan, do, review' model of learning (see page 25), children can begin to reflect on working style and learn to judge the effectiveness of their efforts

18 Tell it straight and straight away

For best effect, praise should be given straight, with no ifs and buts, no sarcasm, no reminders of past failures or other put downs to dilute its effect.

And it should be given straight away whenever possible as that conveys spontaneity. Sometimes the positive response does not occur to us at the time, or we are busy with other children so don't really take the relevant information in. A parent who is away for work should be primed to say something appreciative on the telephone that day rather than wait until the homecoming and receive the lists of good deeds that need complimenting. Most girls would rather hear an informal, more genuine comment at the time even if that means it is less well-informed than a measured, serious assessment delivered later.

Better late than never is certainly advisable; but even better to say it sooner rather than later.

Parents

* children take praise very seriously so treat it seriously. It's not the moment for jokes so don't be sarcastic if you want your comments to be effective

* if you didn't respond at the time, make amends by saying something like, 'I thought again about what you told me, properly this time. Sounds like you did really well and it was important. That's terrific'

* say it like you mean it: while you are looking at your child, not as you turn to leave the room

Teachers

* the quicker you can give feedback on work done, the more a girl will learn from your comments because she will still remember how she approached the task and can see both what she did well and what she needs to change

* if you make positive comments on children's personalities, interests, sociability and style, these can be given straight away

19 Focus on the achievement, rather than on her

'Focus on the behaviour, not the child' is recommended by most parenting pundits. It is fundamental, and as relevant to giving praise as to meting out discipline and punishment when the golden rule is usually promoted. Separating children from their behaviour makes so much sense in relation to discipline. Letting a child know she's loved – that we're just not wild about what she's done – allows every child to hold on to that all-important sense of self-worth that feeds self-respect and the will to do well.

In relation to praise, we should always focus on what it is our daughter has achieved, not on who she is. 'That was terrific, what you managed to do' is a far less emotionally entangling thing to say than 'you're so wonderful to have got that far / done that. I love you so much!' She may not feel so wonderful, knowing full well she didn't pull out all the stops for this event. She may realise, too, that you tell her off when she has been naughty so she knows she is not always so wonderful. We should love and feel proud of our daughters all the time, not only when they have done well.

Parents

* girls under three cannot separate what they do from who they are, so very young girls need it very simple. Approval words that mention the achievement will be enough, such as 'Well tried!', 'Eating all your dinner was great', 'Great catch!', 'Lovely picture', 'Good job to wait your turn'

* from about aged ten, girls feel more emotionally independent. They no longer want much public display of affection because they are trying to be free. Surprise hugs are great, but praise should always commend the achievement, not her. 'That was a clever thing to do' not, 'You are so clever'

Teachers

* girls may like to feel liked, as in accepted and enjoyed, by their teachers but they tend not to relish favouritism or personal comments. 'Jane always gives her work in on time' is easier to accept than 'Jane's the only reliable girl here when it comes to handing in work'

* 'that exercise you did for me last month was great. That shows you can do it', rather than 'You're really clever, if only you'd believe it. Of course you'll do it fine'

20 Offer good news, bad news choices

I like to hear the bad stuff first, 'cos otherwise it seems even worse. (8)
I like the good news first. Then I can take the bad news better. (8)

There are two parties in any learning situation – the teller and the person being told. To be effective as a mentor, coach or mere supporter, we have to understand how the information we have to offer could be received. Truth and honesty may be what we're ready to give, but if the girl who receives the 'telling' isn't ready to hear that, she can block it by denying or ignoring it.

So if we decide the time has come not to beat about the bush any more, either because she's now older and may not need so much cushioning or because she has started to misjudge herself, we can begin by giving her some control over the level of honesty in any feedback. If we give her the choice of hearing the good news or the bad news first, she's far more likely to remain receptive.

Parents

* be sensitive to the moment: consider the context and recent events. If she's had a tough time and disappointments elsewhere, don't choose that moment to 'give it to her straight'!

* if you have not asked her what she thinks, begin your reply, '*I think you know this already* . . . you were a bit slow off the mark at the start / you weren't turning quickly enough . . .' The point is to reduce her dependency on you

* always ask at the end, 'Did you think my comment was fair?' or, 'Was it useful to hear that?'

Teachers

* check afterwards how your comment was received. 'I was quite honest with you on that. Did it upset you or was it helpful?'

* feedback is a process and learning is a two-way street. Allow and encourage students to reflect and discuss with you how they react to your style and approach. Take class soundings but note individuals' views too

CHAPTER 4

Ages and Stages: Adapting to development

The five separate stages of childhood mark out key changes in children's needs, in what they are progressively able to do, how they are able to think, what they are able to understand and therefore in how they will see themselves. It is clear, then, that parents and teachers need to be sensitive to these changes and adjust their praise style and strategies as girls mature.

Newborn babies are engrossed with their physical needs and very dependent for these on their carer. But they also respond vigorously to close attention and react to it very physically – every bit of their body moves and their whole being seems engaged in the communication. Newborn babies have to face a bewildering array of sounds, smells, signs and behaviours. The challenge for carers is to make them feel physically and emotionally safe through establishing reliable close contact and familiarity through regular routines and patterns.

Sometime during their second year, a baby becomes a walking and talking toddler. These skills make her feel far more independent and her sense of self and gender become clearly established. She will want to explore, experiment and examine everything. Though she's now capable of doing so much more, her dominant experience can be of failure and incompetence as she stumbles and fumbles, breaks things, misjudges things and tries to make sense of the myriad rules that suddenly appear. At this age, girls are generally better coordinated than boys and their better language skills help them to explain why something happened, but a toddler will still need a great deal of tolerance of the inevitable mistakes made during the steepest learning curve of her life. Encouragement for each small step made towards self-management and self-control, tolerance of her frustrations and lots of attention will help her to feel noticed, competent, understood and affirmed.

From the age of four to about seven, girls see life very simply: things are either good or bad or right or wrong, which also means that they see themselves in the same simple terms, as either a good girl or a bad girl. Subtlety is not what they're about or what they see, so parents should think carefully about the balance of positive and negative feedback they give. Most of the time little girls are very keen to please, provided they're not angry about feeling left out or sense they are unloved. They still rely on copying – parents, brothers and sisters – for a lot of their learning, and they need to sense that they're on the right track.

In the pre-teen years, girls may need their parents' approval to give them security and confidence as they jump into the shark-filled waters of friendship. Friends are beginning to matter more and are looked to for affirmation: these girls would prefer to get on with life and not be on constant watch for an adult's approval or disappointment. Tweens are starting to separate, especially from their mothers, are enjoying their growing freedom and paying increasing attention to the views of friends. However, they need lots of positive back-up as they try out a broader range of skills and activities that their stronger bodies allow. At this stage, appreciation for what they can now do is at least as important as approval for who they are.

Teenage girls still value approval, but if praise goes over the top they feel uncomfortable. They enjoy their efforts being noticed and appreciated but they are beginning to judge much more for themselves and know exactly how big a deal any achievement is. As one fifteen-year-old said, 'My dad's not around much and when he is he's usually reading. So it feels like he's not concentrating and it's not so gushing, which I like.' Another said, 'As you get older you don't need information from parents so much. Your teachers know better what's your level. But it's still good to be appreciated.' One issue with teenage girls is that their increasing independence makes it harder to know what they're doing, good or bad. Any inquisition is likely to feel intrusive and make them retreat into themselves or away from their parents. Their very need for more privacy suggests they want parents less and more time alone to work things out for themselves. So lie low, save your celebrations for the notable successes and in the meantime, focus on affirmation. Make sure, too, you don't criticise their views and values, their friends, ideas, clothes, passions or their creativity, all of which are essential parts of their maturing identity.

21 Make babies feel safe and secure

Babies are able to read people long before they can read words. They notice and recognise our moods, tone of voice and physical movements long before they can understand what is being said. They will be more sensitive to these than possibly at any other time of their lives, as it is through recognising patterns in these that they feel linked to our world. Almost from the moment of birth we know that babies copy as a way to communicate because they can poke out the tip of their tongue when someone does it to them at close range. They let us know how they feel through their limbs that either flail in distress or twitch excitedly; and, of course, through crying and smiling. Their cries can express hunger, discomfort, loneliness, boredom or anxiety – any of which an adult might feel. By meeting their need for food, safety, love, warmth and security, we demonstrate that we understand them and their need for us, which is sufficiently affirming to them that we can call it praise. What matters to them is less *what* we say than that we say, or even sing, something to them in tones that are familiar and sound soothing. Simply talking, even out of view, tells them that we are near. Paying closer attention shows that we care and they can rely on us.

Parents

* at this age, attention-seeking is definitely attention-needing. Babies become obviously distressed when someone who is playing with them looks or moves away; and they come alive when adults connect with them directly

* choose a song to sing at each clear stage of their day: to mark feeding, bath time or nappy changing, for example. She will then begin to recognise the tunes and anticipate the daily routines

* holding and carrying her, playing with her nose or chin, fingers and toes establishes and helps her to experience her physical boundary, which provides her first sense of self

Teachers / carers

* one-to-one contact with young babies is very important to ground their sense of being, safety and significance

* regular and reciprocal social, visual and emotional contact and stimulation helps their brains to establish positive neural connections

* routines are vital to give any baby or young child a sense of safety, order and security

22 Babies must feel they're important

As far as anyone can tell, new babies have very little awareness of having a separate identity: they merge with their care giver as one. One key way in which they begin to realise they matter to us and develop that sense of being a significant, important and separate person is to have us be in tune with them and responsive to the signals they send out. Psychologists call this form of give and take, notice and react, style of interacting 'synchronicity' and 'reciprocity'. It is comforting for babies, even at this level, to know that they can communicate, be heard and understood. This is a far cry from the scheduled, over-organised, packaged up and packed off babies that are required to fit in to other people's superimposed and fixed routines – though it has already been said that babies need some routine. To reciprocate implies respect for the growing person and her developing personality. This requires that we look, listen and notice, respond and love and care.

Parents

* allow her to develop her own patterns and pace, and respect these

* babies work very hard to form an intimate relationship with their care giver. If we fail to notice their efforts and ignore them, they will then stop trying and switch off

* playing with her fingers, face and toes; holding her tight and sharing with her the rhythm of our body, as she shares hers with us; and responding to her fears, delights and sufficiency in relation to food, sleep or entertainment, tells her of our deep sense of love and regard for her being and welfare

Teachers / carers

* endeavour to maintain a carer/infant ratio that enables individual infants' patterns to be respected, within a structure that offers familiarity and security

* professional convenience matters, but not if it is acquired at the expense of infant health and contentedness

23 Give your toddler a positive view of herself

Toddling girls have a hard time because they make lots of mistakes and have accidents. They can irritate their parents sometimes beyond measure as they try to carve out space for themselves and strive to be listened to in a family's otherwise busy life, usually by crying, kicking and whining. Living with a toddler can be a constant battle, and if it is, it can be a challenge to say enough positive, affirmative, approving and appreciative things to offset the negative signals we send through shouting, anger, frustration or simply insisting that our will be done. Yet toddlers need to feel loved and successful to thrive, just like older girls.

Even during the 'terrible twos', a girl will not yet have a clear sense of her unique self. She is as she does. When we reprimand her for what she does, applying the behaviour/self rule in order to protect her self-respect, she could still feel personally at fault because she is too young to sense or comprehend the difference.

Physical affirmation, that is plenty of cuddles and close physical contact, will help her get the simple yet strong message of our continuing love and approval despite the hassles.

Parents

* give her plenty of cuddles and physical reassurance, especially after a 'bad patch'. Don't necessarily talk, or just say 'That was a tough day!'

* make a joke to end the arguing: 'How silly we are, fighting like a cat and dog!'

* toddlers experience themselves through action. Encourage self-management in as many tasks as possible to help a growing girl feel positive about her role in your world

* encourage her to dress herself – even if the socks are odd, the T-shirt back to front or the colours clash! Involve her in tasks that don't require perfection, such as watering the garden or decorating biscuits

Teachers / carers

* listening helps very young girls to feel they matter. Ensure each one has someone who has time to hear her point of view

* when small children are herded, they may feel very insignificant

* behaviour talks: what is she saying? Get to the bottom of persistent bad behaviour quickly, before she becomes convinced she is a bad girl

24 Tolerate your toddler's frustrations

Until the age of eighteen months, Katie was a model baby. Then, like a typical toddler, she became defiant and disobedient and hated being told no. Katie often flung herself on the floor, kicking and screaming; she would refuse to get out of her car seat; scream if I got her drink wrong, in the supermarket or when I tried to get her dressed ready to go to my mum's. Then I decided to pay her more attention, not be so strict, let her decide little things and to play with her more. The improvement was dramatic.

Toddlers are trying because they're trying it on – almost all the time. Having been carried, sat, fed, dressed, driven and otherwise 'done to' all their short life, they have recently learned they can be a force to be reckoned with. Toddlers use their expanding vocabulary, stronger bodies and clearer sense of self and purpose to say no and assert themselves – it's an intoxicating power that they use to get noticed, gain some control and feel important.

But toddlers also struggle with frustration because they can still achieve so little. Their ideas race ahead of their bodies and they confront real rules. She feels more grown up, yet she still can't master every task or express complex and powerful feelings. No wonder it's a tough time for everyone involved!

Parents

* don't take her anger personally. She does not hate you or want to get at you – she's just expressing complex and powerful feelings she can't put into words

* express her frustrations for her. 'It must have been hard, being ignored / wanting me to stay with you when I had to leave / being fed up with being told what to do and when to do it, when you felt like staying at home and playing'

* explain to her older brothers or sisters why she feels so frustrated and why that can make her a nuisance to them

* make it clear whenever you can that you know she's not being bad, just finding life hard at the moment

Teachers / carers

* offer chances for girls to play through their frustrations, to dance, bash on saucepans or splash paint on big sheets of paper

* choose stories to read that represent her difficulties, so she knows she's not alone and feels more understood

25 Understand what a schoolgirl can't understand

Most arguments between parents and children happen when children fail to match up to parental expectations. Older children may choose to play in a rock band rather than follow mum or dad into the favoured family profession, but clashes with young children usually occur where children cannot (or don't) think or behave in the way her parents expect, when she is consequently considered thoughtless, selfish, immature or even spiteful.

Girls aged between four and seven or eight are not, and cannot be, grown up. Children develop slowly and in set ways, and some girls develop more slowly than others. 'Don't be such a baby!' is especially humiliating when thrown at girls who will have already picked up that they should be more resilient, reliable, organised, cooperative and less emotional than they are capable of being. Praise should not be conditional on her understanding more than she can. And criticism should not fly when we are frustrated that she fails to think ahead, understand a complicated rule, anticipate consequences or imagine how we or how anyone else will react. Girls of this age are still very self-oriented: they understand others through assuming others will feel and act as they do, yet their self-understanding is still very underdeveloped.

Parents

* when a girl is criticised for falling short, she can easily feel guilty for letting you down and assume there is something wrong with her

* she has to be very grown up and organised at school, so she may want to revert after a trying day and be less responsible at home. Accepting this will demonstrate empathy and understanding

* find as many ways as possible to spend and enjoy time with her

* whatever she believes you think of her tends to be how she views herself. If she knows you enjoy her, find her fun, reliable and capable, she will work and make friends more confidently when these become important

Teachers

* girls can find it harder to fit in and participate in class activities if home life is stressful. Give any temporary 'loner' a special buddy or use paired activities for a while in class rather than larger group ones

* if you feel unsure about the key changes that accompany developmental stages for younger girls consider taking a course or finding a suitable textbook

26 Help her to see who she is

Early childhood is when a girl begins to fill out her idea of who she is and what makes her unique. By the time she reaches seven or eight years old, she will have developed a much clearer sense of what it is she is good at, what her main likes and dislikes are, what and how she prefers to play, how her parents and other adults find her and whether she generally gives pleasure or provokes anger or frustration.

Parents can help a girl to clarify and deepen her identity and ensure it is positive. Instead of simply saying 'I think you're lovely!' we can be far more specific and say 'You are really lovely because you are fun to be with, you are very kind to your friends and share things, you love to paint – even though you hate the cleaning up after, you clearly prefer to learn by trying things out rather than just accepting what you're told'. The more detail we can give, while remaining as non-judgemental as possible, the better she will understand and appreciate herself.

Parents

* make her feel she belongs to a clear family grouping and to you. Arrange family outings and events, tell her about her life as a baby and about what your life was like as a child, and involve her in as many of your commitments as is practical or sensible

* experiment with the concept of a 'personality palette'. The more patches of colour that represent different aspects of her personality, skills and preferences you can help to create, describe and place on her personal palette, the more attractive, colourful and detailed will be the picture she can paint of herself

Teachers

* make sure each child is aware of something – her special passion or a particular skill – she can feel positive and proud of; that will help her to have a clear and positive sense of who she is and her capabilities

* help her to be aware of her personal preferences that will include her preferred working style and her favoured activities and subjects. Cover, too, her favourite food, animal, television programme and so on

27 Encourage your pre-teen's developing skills

When my mum asks if I've learnt anything new at my trampoline class, I can't answer because she doesn't understand anything about it. I'd prefer her to know more. (10)

The pre-teens are renowned as the five years in which children's confidence typically flourishes, as long as peer or school pressures do not grind them down. Their stronger bodies and more capable minds enable girls to view things more reflectively, to be more determined to master complex physical and mental tasks and to work out how to correct mistakes when they get things wrong.

As girls' physical coordination improves, they become far more skilled with their hands. It is the age when they can begin to make clothes for their dolls, enjoy plaiting hair, colour in fine geometric grids to create their own patterns and cut paper more finely and decoratively. It is, typically, the 'arty crafty' period. Of course, they can also climb trees and catch, kick and hit balls better but girls generally love to enjoy and develop their fine motor skills. Feeling more confident about who they are, it is their skills and growing judgement that pre-teen girls love adults to notice.

Parents

* admire her growing competence so she feels proud and capable

* give her chances to demonstrate and develop her newly-acquired skills. Ask her to help you with practical and decorative tasks and appreciate her contribution

* watch her doing something she enjoys, even if it is something you find tedious

* let her be outside and active as much as possible, provided you have gone over appropriate safety rules

Teachers

* skills that can be applauded and encouraged could include artistic, humour, dramatic, academic, social, communication, sporting, manual dexterity, personal organisation, imagination, physical coordination, musical, memory, listening, sound judgement and empathic skills

28 Accept your pre-teen daughter's need to act female

My nine-year-old daughter suddenly developed an interest in really feminine things and wanted to cosy up to her friends' mothers that fitted this stereotype, rejecting me. From having been quite a tomboy she wanted pretty dresses, girlie toys and nail varnish. I was quite upset, being a strongly committed feminist and working mum who wasn't interested in fashion and the like. I seemed to lose her, then; but by the age of fifteen she became an activist like me, supporting all the same causes!

Gender awareness flourishes in the phase between eight and twelve years of age. Girls gradually pull away from their exclusive emotional need for their mothers, as friends rise in significance. Indeed, they explore a variety of female models and stereotypes with their friends, hence the common obsession with celebrity beauties. Their play and interests become very gender-focused and they look down on boys as sub-human beings.

Pre-teen girls typically gather in small cliques and talk endlessly. They can become quite bitchy, and use their sharper tongues and growing verbal confidence to both flatter and suck up to their peers; they also sometimes turn hostile and bitchy to pull rank.

Parents

* try not to criticise her 'girlie' behaviour continuously. She is simply a novice trying on femininity for size to see which outfit's comfortable

* pre-teens need to demonstrate their difference. By understanding her cheeky challenges, you show you approve and accept her

* provided she's not endangered, don't 'dis' her friends or any close female role model who is helping her into womanhood

Teachers

* while they flirt with femininity and fleeting fashions, comment favourably on pre-teen girls' passions and purpose, to indicate these inner, personal characteristics remain important

* appreciate pre-teen girls for who they are: growing people who are desperate to fit in and be accepted. Bossiness often hides deep vulnerability and fear of failure

29 Teenage girls like it measured and moderate

Q: *Do you grow out of wanting to be praised?*
A: *You can't not like it. (15)*

Teenage girls still want to hear praise but it is better to keep it measured and moderate, to avoid the danger of praise dependency and encourage independent working. They are becoming more discriminating and want it real. They certainly don't want to be flavour of the week one day and in the doghouse the next. What teenage girls appreciate most is being noticed and treated as a source of authority about their welfare, future and progress. They need to be trusted before they can fully trust their individual ability to evaluate accurately and therefore do well.

Teenage girls value praise and appreciation more when it is sparing. From parents or teachers alike, they report that when it is in plentiful supply, its value decreases. At this stage girls like parents to be around in the background to provide a sense of stability – and to chat about this and that when the moment seems right.

Parents

* always ask her how she rates her own work, result or performance before you expound, 'That seems a good outcome / result, but it's how *you* judge and see it that matters more'

* ask her if the news is worth passing on, 'Do you want to contact your Dad, or is it not such a big deal?'

* keep it simple: 'Well done', 'That's terrific. Were you pleased?'

* say something at the end of the week rather than every day

* appreciate her views and values more than her daily results so you seem truly interested in and impressed by her rather than obsessed with what she can do

Teachers

* girls enjoy all of a teacher's commendations – they like to be liked – but those that make most impact will be directed at her hard work and progress

* ensure that any favourable comments are well supported with detail so she knows exactly what it is she has done well and she can believe it

* for praise to be truly empowering, it must suggest that she has mastered the process just as much as the individual task at hand. 'You have written a very good essay. You are planning your arguments much better, your conclusions are more complete and you are now weighing different approaches. Great'

30 Give her faith in her future as an adult

Her parents considered her brilliant, but the better she did in sport, music and academically, the more she realised there were others who were superior and she felt a failure. At university she doubted every assignment and thought she would flunk; it was the same during her training and her first year at work. Though she aimed high with great results, she could not accept that she deserved her success and that it would continue.

Girls are, by and large, doing well. Self-esteem questionnaires show girls at their lowest ebb at the age of thirteen but with rising confidence from then on, unlike boys who live on chutzpah and bravado through childhood and reach their low point at the age of nineteen when they can no longer pretend. But there are still too many girls who lack confidence and can't quite believe they have the qualities to go far when they face tougher competition.

Parents can help by commenting favourably on their daughter's growing maturity and general competence, on her time management and problem-solving skills, rather than continuing to highlight specific exam results that make the success temporary and possibly unconvincing.

Parents

* understand the continual uncertainty she may face

* make her believe her destiny is in her hands, 'Just look at your past. You're clearly capable of getting to wherever you decide to go. The future is yours. And whatever path or career you decide, we'll back you'

* show respect for her ideas, plans, views and values and assume that others will respect her too. Ultimately, these will be more powerful survival tools than her final results, so reduce the heat on these

Teachers

* encourage teenage girls to look and plan ahead and commend their past achievements as well as being positive about their plans

* invite previous pupils to return to describe their personal journeys

* mentors can help enormously to boost individuals' confidence and focus on the possibility of a brighter future than might otherwise be assumed

CHAPTER 5

What to Notice and Encourage: Being creative

It is good practice to find at least three things about our children to notice and comment on positively every day and we should use that comment to point to the past, the present and the future. You should not be asking *if* a child is good at anything, but 'what is my child good at?' because it is undoubtedly true there will be something about what she says or does to notice and appreciate. We just have to be thoughtful and creative.

It is often said that it takes four 'praises' to undo the negative impact of one criticism, so how often we should, or need, to say something encouraging and endorsing depends in part on how critical we have been. Clearly there needs to be a limit: if we say five hurtful or undermining things in one day, then trying to say twenty positive statements that same day to even those out becomes logistically difficult (because we don't necessarily spend that much time together), very confusing for our daughter (because we seem to be blowing hot and cold) and can create an atmosphere that is far too intrusive and contrived (because we have to watch so carefully to spot when to pop in the praise). The older girls become, the less they need or want wall-to-wall praise though, of course, it still pleases them when they hear it. Encouragement will become more necessarily context-bound, for example focused on a time of particular challenge. Provided we don't lay it on thick, girls will come to value these less frequent endorsements and appreciations more highly. Don't forget, though, to continue saying how much you enjoy her company and love who she is. The world ahead of her can seem challenging, even frightening, and she'll need every ounce of confidence she can muster.

There is a vast range of possible attributes and achievements to notice. If we focus on a single area, for example school marks and work, we have to ask about these every day in order to know what to say. And whichever aspect of her life we notice most could become the part of her she feels we value most, and the one she would choose to sabotage if she ever feels the desire to hurt us.

If we pride ourselves on offering a tolerant, warm and accepting home, we will value, notice and openly appreciate: all aspects of each child's personality – fears and foibles as well as robustness; skills and talents; general capability; attitude towards others and the ability to deal with problems.

31 Appreciate her thinking skills and opinions

It was an interschool debate on some aspect of history in the curriculum all students present had been studying. The girls who had the confidence to participate were so often timid, hesitant, found it hard to stand tall and straight and were generally unconvincing, even though we had all prepared well. The boys, by contrast, oozed confidence and presented their arguments boldly. They made you believe them. When our history teacher pointed this out, we all had to agree she was right. Final year secondary school student.

Thinking before acting comes more naturally to girls; they are generally better at thinking ahead, considering consequences and understanding emotions which helps them to anticipate how others – friends, parents or 'victims' – will react. Girls, though, particularly when they get older and when they're in the company of boys, are reluctant to shape these thinking skills into firm opinions backed by clear arguments. Perhaps because they have had more experience of being considered 'good' and have basked in that glory, they are less ready to chance a challenging point of view, delivered with confidence, with which others may disagree. Yet this is a quality all girls need to nurture if they are to make their mark in their adult working life.

Parents

* encourage her to voice opinions. Chat about recent hours or days and recall what has happened that she might have found fun, scary or difficult. 'It's interesting you've mentioned that. Why did you find it scary?'

* invite her to plan and think ahead when there's free time to fill or there's an unfamiliar situation to face

* value her choices: 'That's a good idea of what to play!', 'I like how you put that jumper and those trousers together'

Teachers

* encourage girls to speak out and feel confident in doing so: ask questions such as, 'Who's a good problem-solver here?' or 'Let's have another point of view on this. Don't be shy. All views count!'

* write encouraging comments on her work: 'I very much liked your ideas about what Jodie was really thinking in that story'

* ask her how she would have liked a story or game to end, to stimulate flexible thinking and ideas

32 Encourage sociability and standing up for herself

Girls are natural talkers and seek more intimate friendships so are thought to be better adjusted socially and less likely to be loners. The research tells a different story, for one study showed that one in seven children consider they have few or no friends. It is also true that successful and genuine friendships demand some very sophisticated skills that don't always come naturally. They certainly benefit from being oiled and practised at home.

There is a difficult balance to be struck, between girls learning to accommodate, compromise, be flexible and respect other people's points of view, all of which aid friendships, and being able to stand up for themselves – not always going with the flow simply to prove membership and loyalty.

Social and friendship skills start at home. If we show our daughters respect, talk to them frequently and give then plenty of time and attention, they will feel not only that their views matter but also that they are liked so others will like them. And if we ignore our daughter's complaints and disagreements, she'll be less likely to challenge friends when it is safer that she does so.

Parents

* value a range of skills that will help her in social situations, such as empathy, understanding, kindness, sharing and managing arguments without trouncing off

* expect that she joins you sometimes when you visit friends and relatives

* try to have at least one family meal each week to encourage conversation and friendly banter

Teachers

* girls tend to enjoy group work, but sometimes they can use it to shirk accountability and find it comfortable that they're not required to defend a personal view. Both styles of learning – individual and group – should be part of any structured learning process to benefit both girls and boys

* groups of both mixed and same-gender help girls and boys to appreciate each other's strengths and learn from each other

33 Acknowledge that she tried hard

Did you try hard and do your best? That's what matters.

Acknowledging effort is not a soft option, for progress is made at every stage on the learning journey. Getting there is at least as important as arriving; and each arrival point becomes a past staging post from which the learner moves on. It can represent a bigger step forward for someone to realise finally what she's been doing wrong and work out for herself how to correct it than to get something right at the first attempt but with little awareness of why it was correct. It strengthens girls if they know they can work their way through a difficulty.

Effort is important. No one achieves anything significant without it. Effort is something accomplished involving concentration; it means you give it your all. Young children find it hard to concentrate and they will probably have a poor appreciation of what 'trying hard' actually means. But if a young girl's more limited efforts are not respected and valued, it may be harder for her to make the necessary effort when she's older and has more control over it and when the results might matter more.

Parents

* ask her what she means when she says, 'But I tried really hard' before you condemn it as a weak excuse

* ask for specifics such as: time spent on it, amount of any diversion such as TV, computer or phone calls, whether she took the time to look something up if she wasn't sure or whether she checked it over

* if you have every reason to trust her and she said she did her best, not knowing how to do it differently, let it rest at that

Teachers

* do you encourage your students to understand what the terms 'effort' and 'trying' mean?

* do you talk about how difficult it can be to persevere, and what students think and feel when they get despondent? Ask anyone who finds a way through when discouraged to describe what he or she does to achieve this

34 Organisation matters but 'good enough' is also okay

I don't mind that the boys' work is messy or not very fluent, provided they have shown they understand the content. It's the girls who worry me when they underline headings in different colours and make their work pretty as a picture. It's such a waste of their time and so unnecessary. They need to relax a bit. Secondary school science teacher.

Girls tend to be more responsible and self-organised than boys, but they may attach too much importance to being neat and tidy and correct in pursuit of being 'good'. Girls develop a healthier attitude to work and themselves if they can let go and avoid investing their self-worth in each and every assignment.

If poor personal organisation becomes a genuine handicap, we can comment favourably on small examples of organisation and self-management. Tidying just a corner of a bedroom is progress; returning for an item remembered at the last minute is better than forgetting it altogether; and prioritising commitments on a busy Saturday shows forward thinking.

Parents

* suggest strategies to aid her organisation, such as making lists, or writing reminders on sticky notes

* ask her how she prefers to remember things. It must become her project, not yours or it may not work

* notice when she manages to think and prepare ahead; don't demand perfection

* she may be organised in some spheres, just not in the ones you'd like so spot the positive signs!

* a heavy emphasis on tidiness and order could hamper creativity, so seek a balance

Teachers

* discourage pristine and pretty work, even though it may be easier to read. Homework should be functionally correct, not a time-consuming work of art

* a focus on meta-learning – learning how to learn – will automatically encourage girls to consider their procedures and preparation and the trade-offs between time spent preparing work perfectly and having some fun or learning more things

* teach girls the 80:20 rule – that making something 20 per cent better often requires 80 per cent more time, which is not time-efficient. 80 per cent of quality is usually achieved in the first 20 per cent of time spent

35 Value her imagination, however fanciful!

I'm a famous dancer. Everyone wants to come to watch me leap and twirl. But one day I fall on stage and hurt myself so badly that I go dead white and lie as if dead. Someone in the audience jumps down from the balcony to try to revive me, using special powers. He gives me a magic kiss and I come to life again. He falls in love with me immediately and I dance across the stage with joy!

A girl's imagination represents her. It is her own personal creation and not only gives her a sense of freedom but also some productive control over her time. Fantasy allows endless possibilities: she can explore the rare experience of feeling powerful because she can create stories in which she takes a lead role and she has unlimited strength. Being in charge of the story, nothing can go wrong for her unless she so wills it, so she can feel totally safe. If we join in on her terms and accept the role she wants us to play, she in effect is in charge of us too which will help her to accept our bidding much of the rest of the time.

Fantasy encourages mental flexibility and creativity, both of which aid schoolwork. We should appreciate and value her ability to draw, play and explore imaginatively and occasionally enter her fantasy.

Parents

* don't devalue any imaginative play. It is part of her, gives her great skills and increases her self-knowledge and confidence

* girls explore imagination through fiction and fantasy – often romantically tinged as they mature. At the start they play schools, then stories from adventure books or television series and later imagine themselves in liaisons.

* if you join in an imaginative game of hers, don't suddenly talk about the shopping you need to do or what she'd like for tea as it will shatter her creation and belief that you take her seriously

Teachers

* fanciful imagination can become distracting, but girls need to be able to be themselves and be encouraged to take risks with possibilities

* girls' imagination sometimes appears in the form of humour or silly stories. To keep it contained, try to find clear times when students are able to play imaginatively with ideas and allow them to edge towards naughtiness

36 Enjoy her humour

Humour is a chief joy in life. Around the age of seven or eight something very important happens to the way children's minds work. They can look at themselves from the outside, think in abstract categories far more easily and can play with ideas and see new links. Any parent of a girl of this age will tell you that it is at this time they constantly get asked to laugh at weak jokes that their daughter considers utterly hilarious. Children's joke books tend to be pitched at this age group. They repeat jokes heard in the playground which they cannot possibly understand yet they find an alternative explanation that makes sense to them. But it's not just the jokes themselves they enjoy; they take great delight in entering that hitherto closed adult world of joke telling and being in the powerful position of making other people laugh.

Once we laugh the show can go on, and on, and on. It gives her huge pleasure to entertain in this way and makes her feel so proud. We must play the appreciative audience and allow her to exercise her new mental muscles and have fun playing with ideas and words.

Parents

* be patient, and try to laugh – or groan – when you are told a joke even if you have heard it plenty of times before

* magic tricks are visual jokes that play with the viewer's perceptions and expectations. Encourage any interest in magic, and be tolerant of the performance that she may want to arrange for the family

Teachers

* from the age of eight or so, children can begin to understand the real humour of jokes and enjoy telling jokes and making them up. Girls' humour should be valued and brought out, even if it is the boys in the class that hold the stage most of the time. Of course, everyone needs to learn that there are good times for being silly and times when it needs to be vetoed

37 Welcome creativity – and the risks and mess involved

Every human being has the capacity to be creative. Young children find it easiest, because they have less of an idea of what is expected or what is right and wrong. For them, experimentation is fun and helps them to feel in charge and powerful – free from rules and other restrictions. They have not yet absorbed gender-related social conventions, so all can be encouraged to try out a wide range of activities.

When children express their creativity in less organised ways, we should not devalue it simply because it seems to lack purpose. Building outdoor camps, playing hairstyles with generously adorned dolls, mucking about creating dance routines or making up rules for a variety of games are all creative pursuits.

Creativity is the expression of originality: it helps children to discover their identity and experience directly the ways in which they are unique.

Parents

* for girls who are artistic, offer plenty of opportunities to carry on drawing, colouring, painting and sculpting for as long as she wishes

* cooking can be very creative; as can sewing, knitting, crocheting or gardening. Many girls express creativity through pinning up posters and photographs in bedrooms or painting lampshades

* collage-style pictures can be created from discarded rubbish, fabric oddments, dried food or from twigs, leaves, petals, plant seeds

Teachers

* children need peace and quiet to become absorbed in something creative. Try to limit the chat as they explore their ideas and discourage the boys from teasing girls' often more thoughtful efforts

* clearing up afterwards helps to instil good organisational habits and encourages a sensible allocation of time. Invite students to gauge how much time is needed

38 Go deep – endorse her values and beliefs

If one purpose of praise is to make a girl feel good about who she is inside rather than rely on a range of external shows of such things as clothes, toys, kit or talents to make her feel comfortable with herself, we need to respect her values and beliefs.

Younger girls will not have developed any consistent system of values for us to appreciate but they do attach great importance to their friendships and their play. They also possess a natural, passionate concern for fairness that we ignore at our peril. Their beliefs are manifest in the sense they make of their immediate world: these form the structure that creates coherence when they face and have to manage confusing events.

From eight or so onwards, girls' ability to think in more abstract and conceptual ways and see things from other people's standpoint encourages many of them to latch on to concerns that focus on others. Whether it is religion, vegetarianism, the developing world or animals, we should endorse each girl's right to develop her own values and interests and respect her beliefs.

Parents

* girls typically develop passions that are more 'touchy feely', unlike boys' more fact-based passions. A girl's passion may include boy bands, horses, drama, dance or sets of books that involve particular characters. Show interest and help her to find out more to endorse her choices and values

* if she develops a passion for animals, it means she cares for creatures that need to be looked after. We should respect this tenderness

Teachers

* try to find out about individual students' passions and values and make reference to these respectfully

39 Appreciate and develop practical competence

Growing children feel such pride each time they conquer something they were not capable of achieving previously. They spend so many years dependent in some way or other it gives them a sense of freedom and autonomy when they grow tall enough, strong enough, dextrous enough and responsible enough to manage themselves or undertake tasks that combine skill and knowledge that can help others.

Spatial skills – seeing how things fit together, being able to re-arrange objects mentally and remember routes, maps and wiring layouts – are boys' forte, but girls benefit from being able to think in this way too. When she is ready, encourage her to read the map while travelling somewhere, play games such as chess and show her how machines work and how to handle electrical devices safely.

Practical skills help a girl to manage on her own, valuable not so much for survival but because autonomy is the ultimate expression of self. Competencies, then, help to define and action our sense of self and boost self-esteem.

Parents

* write down all the things your daughter is good at and likes to do. Think of ways you could put any of these skills to practical use in the home

* if she is too young to be of genuine help, encourage her to come and hold things for you or pass things, and she will learn at the same time

* give her any discarded bit of electrical appliance or other equipment (if safe) when it has broken to take apart and explore

Teachers

* where a student mentions something she has done, made or mended at home, compliment the skill involved. 'Sounds like you're good at that sort of thing. Want a job at my house!?'

* as girls develop their manual dexterity, show how this can be put to practical use. 'Wow, that would make you good at electronics / tuning my guitar / dicing vegetables / getting my baby daughter dressed in the morning!'

40 Go deeper – accept her fears and feelings

When a child cannot be sad or lonely or angry because her parents will not be pleased with her if she is, she will feel she cannot be the person she knows herself to be and she will believe that she is unsatisfactory.
Dorothy Rowe, author and psychotherapist.

A child whose fears and feelings are ignored or denied will not only feel misunderstood but also very alone. Apart from our psychological inheritance, it is our feelings that make us who we are and give us our sense of self. We experience these, often intensely, before we have the vocabulary to describe them and they are our first building blocks. That certain things interest us, upset, frustrate or hurt us, give us pleasure or make us defensive and react selfishly creates our individuality. If we can recognise all her particular moods and characteristics we will demonstrate a deep understanding of her and how she sees her world.

By accepting her dilemmas at her level, she will be free to be and grow; nothing less.

Parents

* accept that her fearful beliefs are real for her. She should not be told girls don't believe that nonsense and should not feel scared of things like monsters, the dark or deep water

* notice her happy moods from her body movements, shining eyes or her bouncy walk, and say, 'You seem very cheerful today. Something nice must have happened. Lucky you!' and let her keep it to herself if she doesn't want to tell you why

* notice her sad moods, too, and accept that she will feel angry, jealous, resentful, lonely or even hate you, and tell her that's natural and okay. Never deny her difficult feelings

Teachers

* many girls are very sensitive and squeamish. Prevent other children in the class from picking on anyone and teasing them for their natural feelings

* learning can be frightening. Accept that some reluctance to try could mask a deep fear of failure, and try to get to the bottom of this. The learning environment must be made safe for girls who lack confidence

* fears and feelings, indeed all strong emotions, make learning difficult. Understand what a girl might be going through in her personal life, what pattern and expectation of relationships she brings into school, and consider how these may affect her

CHAPTER 6

The Language of Praise: Ways to say it, and do it

Human beings communicate in many subtle and less subtle ways. We use words, touch, facial expressions and a range of different physical and symbolic gestures. We often merely sense the pleasure we have given someone through the tone of voice they use or the way they look at us. We often interpret a number of reactions and piece together an overall impression. As adults, we don't always need to have it spelt out every time that someone considers we have done well.

If praise is valuable and worthwhile because it helps girls to feel acknowledged, noticed, approved of, valued, accepted and appreciated as well as helping them to be successful, it follows that there are many ways to bring this about. So it must be the case that praise does not always have to be given in words. As they mature, girls will appreciate the more subtle signs and know we are grateful. Although language is what we tend to use to express our delight, pleasure and surprise when a child has done well, by extending our praise repertoire we will limit the dangers, already noted, associated with spoken praise, and sometimes surprise them, which is always fun!

If children thrive when they are sure we enjoy them, having fun together when they do well is important. We should not make fun of praise or make fun of them by twisting or sending up praise, but the whole family can have plenty of fun discovering different ways to express love and appreciation and finding approaches that are lighter in tone.

41 Keep approval simple

It's nicer if they say lots of different things, not the same thing over and over. And you like it said with expression, so it sounds like they're really interested. (9)

The more we spell it out, the more laboured, false, inappropriate or overdone the praise can become. To avoid a child feeling burdened or uncomfortable and even misunderstood by our outpourings we should, quite simply, keep our expressions of approval simple.

Approval, as has been explained, focuses on the individual. It puts the child in the spotlight, which is why she may squirm if it becomes exaggerated. Appreciation, on the other hand, relates to the task and therefore sometimes needs to be more detailed and specific (though still not disproportionate) so our child knows she can trust our appreciation.

Even praise that describes and reflects back what has pleased us (sometimes called 'descriptive praise') can be kept simple if we say things such as 'Well cycled', 'Well caught', 'Well tidied' or 'Well tried' instead of 'That was clever, how you cycled that tight circle'. Leaving some detail out allows her to decide for herself what it was that was good and makes her less dependent on our assessment and freer to make up her own mind.

Parents

* vary the words, style and response to avoid sounding like a stuck record. Children very quickly switch off and imagine the rest once they hear the intro, especially when we nag. Even repetitive praise gets to sound stale

* try such responses as: 'That's lovely!', 'Brilliant!', 'Well done!', 'That's great!', 'Thanks for doing that', 'That was sensible', 'How thoughtful!', 'What a great idea!'

* if she begins to look at you askance instead of beaming with pride, go easy. Save your comments for something that matters more to her

Teachers

* comments on written work need to be full and explicit but spoken approval can be short. 'I really liked that story / your arguments / the line you took. Take a look at my comments'

* warmer tones of voice and full-hearted attention convey approval too

42 Say it with a smile

When my mum smiles at me, I kind of know. (9)

Sometimes children don't need to hear anything spoken. Beaming smiles are often enough. When they reach the finish line in the school race and turn round to see if we saw their effort or their triumph, a smile and a nod from a distance is all we can give – and it is often more than enough.

Parents

* we can use commercially
available smiley face stickers,
sparingly, as a surprise or
reminder of our love especially
at times we cannot be there.
But make no mistake: these
will be no substitute for the
real thing!

* for a younger girl, we can
draw a simple smiley face on a
small white board or
blackboard in her bedroom
after bedtime for her to find on
waking. But beware of
forgetting to do so if it has
become a nightly routine

Teachers

* smiley faces drawn or stuck
on the end of work shows you
are pleased with the result but
they don't offer useful detailed
feedback where that is more
appropriate

43 Talk with touch

Touch has its own language. It can say so much in such a variety of ways and it need only be fleeting. Touch, for example, is an intimate way to demonstrate an equality of regard and respect. It can express feelings more quickly than words and although it is less precise, it has the great advantage of allowing the receiver to read what she wants – and needs to hear – into it. It is therefore more likely to 'hit home' and satisfy. Touch is certainly less open to misinterpretation than streams of worthy words and is an important gesture of approval, appreciation and giving. Its capacity to convey understanding makes it also serve as a useful way to demonstrate empathy.

A child who lives around adults that never touch her, even if they say the 'right' praise words, will feel ignored, unworthy of attention, inferior, misunderstood and, eventually, ashamed – the very opposite of what we hope praise will achieve.

Parents

* experiment with little touches of appreciation instead of using words

* if touch has disappeared from your relationship with your growing daughter, sit close to her as she watches TV, ruffle or stroke her hair or take her hand and play with it as you chat with her at bedtime

* if she finds your approaches difficult, ask her before you do it so you know she feels ready for it

Teachers

* of course it is not usually appropriate for professionals to touch students, especially as they get older. Nevertheless, if you stand quite close while you look over work, you can show you find her acceptable and feel comfortable in her presence

* consider whether presenting your outstretched palm as athletes do is an alternative acceptable way to demonstrate approval and appreciation

44 Use fun gestures

My teenage daughter did very well in some important exams. I wanted to show my appreciation and acknowledge her achievement without using money, gifts or getting too heavy about it because she'd worked hard for her own satisfaction, not to please me. I bought a large sheet of stiff card, selected a handful of photos from the family collection representing different stages of her life and stuck these on, writing an amusing comment against each one that made reference to her early potential. She thought it was silly but funny and she loved the gesture! She still has it, eight years on.

Money is not the only way to measure value or express pleasure, though it can be very easy to sign cheques. Although girls love to get something new that they have longed for, they also appreciate being on the receiving end of an original gesture that takes time and special effort, something tailored to her passions and which makes her laugh. It will almost certainly be remembered for longer.

Parents

* other fun gestures that can show our appreciation could include:
- arranging a special outing as a treat
- preparing her favourite meal
- having a friend over to sleep
- buying a new cushion, lamp or bedcover for her room

Teachers

* quizzes work well as an end-of-term treat to recognise the class's collective progress. Simple prizes of sweets or chocolate or party bag gifts make it even more fun and special

45 Hugs are for sharing

My teenage daughter got some wonderful SAT scores and I hugged her to share her jubilation; but she clearly wanted it kept brief. I then turned to our dog, told him he was lucky to have such a clever mistress and ruffled his head fondly. She laughed and immediately took him in her arms to receive, as it were, a second appreciative hug.

A hug is a physical gesture that enables us to share any feelings of joy or disappointment. It is essentially non-judgemental because it is empathic and it says, 'I'm happy for you' as well as 'I am sad / happy / pleased with you', in both senses of the phrase. It is a two-way gesture, for the hug has to be accepted and reciprocated. When it finishes, it leaves our daughter holding the feeling and there is nothing we can take away from her and use for our benefit.

Some families don't feel comfortable with such physical closeness. They don't hug much, or kiss or express themselves. As girls enter their teens, they may start to decline intimate parental embraces particularly if she is dating. Passing on a hug from a pet dog or cat, or from a soft toy that's an old favourite, may help to convey an embrace without forcing one on her.

Parents

* 'here's a hug [and make the gesture]. When you're ready for it, come and get it!'

* 'is your happiness for sharing? How about me giving you a hug, then?'

* 'that's made me really happy. Give me a hug so I can share it with you'

* I like getting a hug. Not kissing you though! that's yuck (13)

Teachers

* teachers cannot hug children, but they are able to stand close or pat an arm or shoulder instead or express their delight in words

46 Say it with surprises!

My mum bought a balloon with my name on and put it in my bedroom for when I got home. I felt really special. (10)

Surprises are another way of saying thank you, or showing appreciation or love. A favourite meal, a plate of pieces of fruit arranged as a funny face or an animal, a surprise outing, a balloon that you have written or drawn on, an unexpected small present, are all examples of surprises that can show appreciation of some special effort or simply to say how much you have enjoyed her that week or weekend.

Friday treats are a lovely way to sign off a school week. If any girl wants to know what the treat is 'for', we can reply: to mark the end of a week's work or 'because you are you!'

Parents

* treats and surprises don't have to be earned or deserved

* if a treat is laden with hard-to-earn parental approval, it could make a child anxious and think, 'But what if I'm not good next time?' and so could become tainted

* the pleasure is the surprise and the thought, not the object itself. It can be really simple – and cheap!

* 'today, just for fun, we're going on a mystery night walk with torches!'

Teachers

* curriculum pressures often leave little space for surprises but the end of term is a good moment to appreciate everyone's commitment and have fun together

47 Let her feel what ever she feels

My six-year-old daughter's school report was very complimentary. Her teacher was especially positive about how well she was doing academically. When I said, 'Well done', she buried her face and choked, 'It's a stupid report. What's the point of saying I'm good when it's so easy?'

Affirmation means we accept her as she is, not fashioned according to what we want to see because that makes life simpler. A girl who does well and thrives (for these are not the same things) is someone who knows herself and feels free to 'be'. If she feels able to feel sad, frustrated, happy, disappointed, angry, hateful, confident, frightened or excited, she will probably experience her parent's tolerance and continuing presence and love throughout all these as a sign she can trust them, and herself, because they accept and trust all of her. She will feel understood, and if given the scope to decide when she pulls out the stops, when she coasts, when she explores her developing interests and how she uses and allocates her time, she will be sufficiently confident to manage this sensibly.

Parents

* our feelings are the building blocks of our selves

* allow her to feel disappointed or angry if she doesn't do well – or if anything that you say doesn't go down very well

* if you take the time and trouble to understand the feelings that may explain her behaviour, you will find out more about her

* it is normal for girls to feel angry, insulted, hostile and proud, for girls are, like us, whole human beings. Ask yourself why her reactions bother you; don't put the pressure on her to deny or ignore them

Teachers

* acknowledge girls' feelings, though ensure that the rules about acceptable ways for these to be expressed are maintained

48 Allow her to say it

It is not necessarily pig-headed or offensively arrogant for a child to believe she has done well and admit so. Indeed, secondary school students are increasingly encouraged to judge the quality of their own work as part of well-organised self-assessment programmes. Many nursery schools, influenced by recent government guidance, invite children as young as three to 'plan, do, then review' the effectiveness of their chosen approaches to various tasks.

The possible downside of openly admitting to having been successful is pride and conceit. Children quickly identify 'stuck up' braggers and can turn against them ruthlessly; indeed, most children possess a deep-seated reticence about their talents and are not natural boasters. Perhaps those who do simply copy their parents! But the danger is avoided if we make clear that her particular abilities do not make her better as a person than someone without those talents and that she should never look down on anyone who performs differently. The knowledge that she's done her best and is doing well at whatever activity should stay private to her.

Parents

* teach that 'good at' means 'different from' not 'better than' in anything other than comparative skill terms

* always ask, 'Are you pleased with it?' or 'Would you praise this?' and let her decide and say it

* girls tend to underestimate their work in self-assessment. If she says it's not good enough and she's not happy with it, ask what she thinks is wrong or weak and also what's good. She may then be encouraged to be less self-critical

Teachers

* 'I was very happy with this. Well done. Did you think you'd done it well?'

* encourage self-assessment, backed up with peer review and peer moderation

* before you write the end of term report, ask students to anticipate your remarks. If there is a major discrepancy between your view and a student's, in either direction, discuss it with her later

49 Let siblings in on it

It feels like the older ones get all the praise even if they don't, because they're doing important exams. You automatically feel less special. (11)

It is part of being in a family that siblings value and appreciate each other's special achievements. Praise shouldn't always be issued from the top down. Whereas no child should have to take over a parent's responsibility for affirming or accepting a brother or sister; each child will feel more generous and open with praise and less threatened by or possessive of it where there is a genuine sharing around of family appreciation and praise is not treated as a treasured winner's cup or instrument of advantage to exploit.

Difficulties can arise where one sibling has talents or interests that enable her to be more enthusiastic and all-round successful than another. She may then attract more admiration from friends and family, creating an imbalance between siblings. If this happens, ask the surrounding admirers to cool off and make sure the others receive plenty of loving attention and appreciation, often more nourishing than accolades. Be careful, too, not to blur the line between the achievement and the child as this may increase jealousy and rivalry.

Parents

* show joy in each of your children's varied milestones, pleasures and personalities

* younger siblings can draw a picture as a gesture for their sister if she does well. Older ones can say, simply, well done, spend a little bit of time talking about the event and come to watch the dance, play, match or event a younger sister may be involved with

* don't allow one child in particular to get all your acclaim and attention. If there is potentially destructive jealousy, the balance that you seek to achieve could become upset

* view a child's talent as 'her chosen thing' rather than as anything remarkable

Teachers

* positively value each child as an individual

* raise the suggestion that a sibling in the same school might like to know about some special outcome

* beware actually telling a brother or sister about their sibling's good efforts, in case it is misinterpreted as an underhanded incentive to improve

50 Watch out for 'I' phrases

Praise should focus more on the event or the child than on us. Once we start sentences with 'I . . .' the emphasis becomes our view of things. 'I like the way. . .', 'I'm very pleased', I think you could have done more to . . .' 'I was surprised you did so well . . .', 'I am convinced everything will go well for you because you have prepared so thoroughly'. The earlier discussion of the purpose of praise highlighted such things as acknowledgement, attention and affirmation. Children love to please their parents when they are young, but as they get older they need less parental pleasure and more affirmation and confirmation that they have judged things well and are on the right track, which will encourage confidence.

If a girl is hungry for praise she will find any format rewarding, including all 'I . . .' phrases, but these won't help to wean her off any unhealthy reliance on our judgement. If she starts to sense she is being manipulated or too closely monitored, she may simply ignore them all. On the other hand, phrases such as 'You did really well', 'That was a brilliant result' or 'The way you were able to reflect on that exam paper and spot where you went wrong was impressive', are more focused on the process and are statements of fact that centre on her, not of judgement that centre on you.

Parents

* 'you are lovely as you are, *and* you're extra special to me!' is less loaded than 'I love you as you are' – especially if she has just done something to please you

* 'you handled that really well. Others might have lost their cool. Well done!' is preferable to, 'I really liked the way you handled that'

* 'you're such fun to be around' is less of a burden to carry than 'I love being around you when you're this cheerful'

* free her: focus your remarks on her ability to set about tasks well rather than offering your opinion on the outcome

Teachers

* 'you've clearly got the measure of this problem now. This was a terrific assignment and shows what you are really capable of' is more convincing than, 'I am pleased you have understood this problem and done this piece of work so well'

CHAPTER 7

Common Mistakes to Try to Avoid

Despite the best of intentions and our wish to help girls do well and show how much we love and appreciate them, we can still either say the wrong thing entirely or say the right thing at the wrong time or in the wrong way and, through clumsiness or ignorance, put our foot in it.

Though it may surprise some people, the worst offence is not necessarily criticism, some of which may be justified and valuable. It is not helpful to protect our child from every nuance of disapproval or disappointment. When she has misjudged or failed to understand things or ignored clear guidance, she should receive straightforward yet constructive explanations of what she can do differently next time. Constructive criticism is a far more helpful response than alternatives such as harsh punishment, scathing sarcasm, turning a 'blind eye' or offering fulsome praise for effort even if the outcome was way below expectation – and your daughter knows it. These can all have counterproductive consequences and are explored in this chapter.

The dangers that are associated with the wrong kind of attention, be it indiscriminate praise or constant criticism, include perfectionism (explored in Chapter Ten), stress-inducing pressure, burn-out and opting out and, perhaps curiously, feelings of low self-worth. We might intend that our daughter feel pride and satisfaction, but this is not guaranteed. These outcomes, admittedly, lie at the extreme end; signs of interim difficulty or more serious trouble ahead can include secretiveness, mild cheating and copying of other people's work and learned helplessness.

The characteristic common to all the mistakes reviewed here is placing our concerns and desires before our daughter's feelings and wishes: a failure to treat her as an autonomous human being. Each child should, then, be allowed to be who she is and not be compared to anyone else or used by us as a vehicle to make good any missed opportunities of our own that we may now regret. She should be given the freedom to say no or stop and be offered every opportunity to do well for her own pleasure, not simply to please us. Young children, naturally, need more direction and should not have total responsibility for their growth and learning. With older girls, though, parents often need to step in temporarily to help a child over a sticky patch (for example not understanding some mathematics or wanting to give up a musical instrument) but when the problem has been overcome we should then withdraw.

51 Think about why you're saying it

When we consider whether to give what we may see as the 'gift' of praise, we look first at what our child has done and whether the behaviour or circumstance warrants it. Our focus is therefore on her and is context bound, time-limited and top-down: the conscious part of our attention is fixed on her. But less obvious ulterior motives often lurk behind our apparently altruistic actions or comments that have more to do with us – our dreams, desires and fears – than with her. We applaud certain attributes to help her achieve aims we consider desirable. We can so easily try to turn her into what we want her to be.

At one level, this is inevitable. Of course it is a parent's job to encourage socially acceptable behaviour and discourage actions that set her back or will get her into trouble. We do shape children's behaviour and should do so, as gardeners prune growing plants so they develop stronger stems and larger flowers. But we should be careful not to graft on a cutting taken from ourselves or cut and style so much that they need walls or wires to shore them up. We should not contrive to bolster our own vulnerable self-worth with our daughter's success, or fail to give her the autonomy she needs.

Parents

* consider if you are making a point of being positive to compensate for being very preoccupied recently. Could you be saying 'the right things' to make her feel more loving towards you because you need more support?

* if the answer to either of these is 'yes' or 'possibly', beware your motives and manipulation. Better to address the issue directly or at its source

* watch carefully how she responds to the different ways in which you express approval and delight

* as much as you can, put it back to her: 'Yes, I do like it, but the more important thing is whether you do', 'To me, you did very well, but were you pleased with the result?'

Teachers

* if praise is natural, it will trip off the tongue without much forethought

* individual girls who have a despondent personality may need more encouragement than others

52 Ban the word 'good'; it does girls no good

'Good' is such a bad word when it comes to ensuring that praise is effective. It is bad because it is inadequate, for it says so little. It is a shorthand word used to convey many things and sometimes some not very helpful things. It is also bad because it automatically conjures up the idea of the opposite, which is 'bad'; if a girl is not told she is good, the inference is that she is, or could be, bad when she is not being good. 'Good' and 'bad' are not just black-and-white words – they are black *or* white words. When a 'good' girl is being less obliging, or is just behaving normally, she will often be called 'bad', which is neither fair nor beneficial to learning. Girls may decide that striving to be good to please others is the best strategy for them because it is the safest. But this may make a girl unwilling to take risks and discover her true capabilities.

One use of the word 'good' is, 'Good, you did what I wanted you to do and you behaved in the way I hoped you would.' A good child may therefore tend to be passive: is not noisy, boisterous, messy, curious or clumsy and does not break things. She is that particular parent's perfect child. And that's the point. Girls who are encouraged to be good can lose their sense of individuality and identity as they fill the mould shaped by their parents' expectations

Parents

* instead of 'good' we can say clever, organised, thoughtful, helpful or creative; or just say, 'You're a happy girl'. If she has done something she's pleased with, that's what she'll be feeling

* instead of labelling her 'bad' or 'naughty' we should turn it around to our view. 'I found that rather selfish', 'I didn't like that behaviour'

* to convey our delight in her, we can say, 'You're my lovely girl!' which suggests she is very lovable, the pre-requisite for positive self-esteem

Teachers

* 'very good' on a piece of work tells the student very little about what she did right and she may not be sure of this. Instead you could write, 'Very well argued', 'Very well remembered', 'Very good use of detail', 'Lovely description – I saw it all!'

* 'good' girls should be not so good to teach. Really impressive students will inevitably question and challenge academically as well as deliver

53 Don't turn your dream into her success – or nightmare

I told her, I don't care if you fell and smashed your nose. Your ice skating is your job and you've just got to get up again and get on with it. Mother of a nine-year-old ice-skating starlet when her daughter fell during practice. The mother had also skated competitively as a child but had given up before reaching the top.

Being successful does not necessarily generate psychological health and confidence, as we see in the tips on perfectionism. Where girls are required to carry and make a reality of their parents' dreams, they are not usually free to take things in a direction or at a pace that suits them, mix and match their free-time activities to create a better balance, or decide when they have had enough. For success to create confidence and security rather than anxiety and insecurity, girls must believe they are following their own wishes. Mothers and fathers must beware that gymnastics or ice dancing really is just for fun and not to make up for their own near miss in the competitive stakes; or be clear, for example, that tennis coaching is laid on so their daughter may have possibilities to explore, exploit and enjoy, rather than to fulfil a parent's dream or, worse, to generate generous prize money for their personal longer-term financial gain.

Parents

* girls are not puppets – they are growing people

* 'who is she doing it for – for her or for me?' is a very important question that should be asked at every stage of a girl's progress if she is performing competitively. And answer it honestly

* don't compete with, criticise or ridicule her. Every challenge drags her into your territory and reinforces her belief that your view and preferences must be better

* give her room to be herself. It's your problem, not hers, if you feel uncomfortable with her preferred interests and direction

Teachers

* vary your teaching style and lessons. Your comfort zones, passions and communication methods may not suit all the girls in your class

* encourage tolerance and mutual respect for difference between all students so they learn not to impose their values and choices on others

54 Don't take the credit for her success

Sometimes parents invest so much of their time and effort in helping their daughter to achieve the hoped-for success that they are convinced it could never have been achieved without them. They may have spent hours coaching her or sacrificed a great deal to pay for specialist tuition; they may have imposed strict practice regimes or been genuinely supportive when something went awry that a child was able to find her own way back to confidence through tolerance. This enables parents to take responsibility for the success, expressed either privately or openly, which can then underrate their daughter's contribution. Offering rewards and incentives can have the same effect, making parental intervention the critical factor. When parents steal some of the credit, which is what this amounts to, a child may feel empty and used simply as a tool to generate a parent's self-esteem.

Comments such as: 'I told you that you were a "natural", that's why I signed you up for the course' or, 'Congratulations for getting into the team. Aren't you pleased now that I put you on that healthier diet?' clearly claim some of the credit.

Parents

* pass your possible part over to your daughter: 'You became so much more organised. Good job', 'When you started to look after yourself and care about your health it really paid off', 'You took real advantage of the extra experience that course gave you', 'You've developed a lovely relationship with books and it probably helped'

* if your friend's daughter does particularly well at something, it is more appropriate to say, 'I hear Juanita did really well; she must be delighted' than to congratulate your friend and feel jealous

Teachers

* credit the class or individual, not yourself. If you helped, that is no more than your professional duty

* 'I was just the fertiliser – you put down the roots and did the growing!'

55 'I'm so proud of you!'

Which of the following would you be most likely to say? 'I'm really proud of you for managing that!'; 'I hope you feel proud of yourself for doing that – you deserved to do well after all that effort'; 'You probably feel really proud to have achieved that'; 'I feel so proud of you and proud to have you as my child'.

A group of teenagers agreed that the parental phrase they most love to hate was, 'I'm so proud of you'. They found it hard to explain why this response grated so much; but the problem seemed to relate to it being 'over the top' as well as causing discomfort with having a parent too emotionally involved in their work. They did not want the responsibility for delivering or maintaining their parent's sense of pride and they certainly had not worked hard for a particular test or exam in order that their parent could feel that way – they had done it for themselves and for their own reasons.

Our role should be to enable our daughter to feel proud, independently and regardless of our feelings because she knows what she set out to achieve and the effort that she needed to apply.

Parents

* keep comments as free from judgement as possible. 'You probably felt really proud when you heard that' implies that if she did feel that, you can understand why. If not, no matter

* even, 'I hope you feel proud of that result' implies that if she doesn't, she should, because your view counts

* pride can be an overweening opinion: be careful you're not exaggerating her achievement

* pride might, indeed, come before a fall if, as a result of your insistence that she excel in an activity, she decides to reject the pressure and drop it

Teachers

* you can be proud of the achievement of a class – proud of everyone or of your professional input; but your pride is less relevant to any individual's success

* 'I am really impressed with your progress', 'You deserve to feel proud of your achievement' or 'I'm so pleased you have understood things and can now work closer to your true ability level' are more appropriate remarks for individual students

56 Keep it clean: no sarcasm or caveats

Ninety-nine per cent. That's not bad! But why did you let one get away?
The comment of a mother to her sixteen-year-old daughter.

When adults are chary of giving praise, they often lace it with something rather nasty – a sting or kickback – to qualify and downgrade the compliment and make it not quite the generous gesture it might have been. It is a sufficiently common practice that it has been given a name: 'contaminative praise'. It can become a style or habit, is sometimes dressed up as humour and is not always said to hurt; yet it usually does. The child is not quite let off the hook and still needs to wait for the full approval that frees her to move on.

Contaminative praise is probably uncomfortably familiar. Examples of such comments include, 'This school report is great, but why did you have to take so long to mend your ways?', 'That model is really lovely – no one would know you used to be all fingers and thumbs!', 'Your bedroom looks so much tidier now; terrific, but it won't stay this way long – you'll see!'

Parents

* imagine praise as a biscuit: would you give your daughter one as a reward then, just as she reaches for it, pull it back, shake salt onto it and then return it for her to eat? So why would you effectively do that with praise?

* sarcasm is said to be the lowest form of wit

* if you see it as harmless fun, reflect on the essence of humour. Is making jokes at other people's expense – especially children who won't see it the same way – the only way to have fun and make others laugh?

Teachers

* sarcasm is neither an effective nor a professional tool for teachers. It should never be used as it confuses and humiliates

57 Absence makes children's hearts grow harder

My two-year-old daughter was looked after by a neighbour's daughter during the day when I took a short-term job. She was great, devising many activities. But then she went off to university. She turned on the charm and enthusiasm very naturally on her first return visit and my daughter loved it, but after each absence thereafter she became increasingly confused, finally turning away.

For adults, so the saying goes, absence makes the heart grow fonder. This is not the case for children, who find unexpected or longer absences due to work trips or hospitalisation much harder to understand and endure because they need to trust and rely on people for their security. Young children in particular are likely to feel at least a little bit abandoned, unwanted or at fault when, for example, they start day care and it is unfamiliar. Largely because they are extremely egocentric, they often believe the absence must be a punishment for a wrongdoing.

We sometimes cover our guilt for periods of absence by being extra attentive, fawning and over-rewarding them when we return. This may console a child for a while, but then could confuse and bother her so she stops trusting the praise.

Parents

* if you have to be away frequently, develop clear and predictable routines and rituals that mark your leavings and your returns so she can learn to predict and trust your love despite your absence

* try not to be over-exuberant when you come home, especially if you expect to be away again soon or be very pre-occupied, which can amount to the same thing. A calm, intimate, tight cuddle may be more effective than bellows of delight with multiple presents

Teachers

* if you have had to take time off from the classroom at unpredictable moments, don't expect your fulsome feedback to have quite the same positive impact when you return. It takes time to rebuild the trust

* girls who have felt rejected and constantly criticised or manipulated by their parents may reject any form of appreciation or approval from their teachers because they will find it hard to accept it as truth

* for disbelieving students, select one thing only to comment positively on and mention this six times every day. Eventually, she will begin to see herself differently and accept that she is worthy of appreciation

58 Accentuate the positive – but notice the negative

When you're upset about something that hasn't gone well, I'd prefer they tell you what they really think, instead of just saying it was fine and it doesn't matter. (11)

It is fine to accentuate the positive, especially when girls are young; but as they get older the negative should increasingly be noticed, not ignored. A young girl will make lots of mistakes; it is hard for her to think ahead, rules are hard to grasp and she will get tired, fractious or need attention. We should understand and tolerate these errors that cannot really be considered 'naughty' and we should certainly not punish her. At a period of life when mistakes and accidents abound she should be allowed to start her life feeling positive, capable and confident, not cowed by constant criticism and failure.

But by the time girls reach the age of six or seven, the negatives should be noted and addressed. 'Accentuate the positive' means, essentially, to emphasise helpful behaviour and to make it conspicuous, but that does not mean we should ignore outrageous behaviour or go overboard with overdone exaggerations when the event is modest.

Parents

* 'I love going with you to the shops but this time it was not fun. It's not okay for you to go on and on about having something to eat or to nag about missing your TV programme. You're usually great company, but I'll think about going alone if it happens again'

* 'I prefer to hear "At least you tried hard, even if you didn't do so well" rather than "good" which is false' (15)

* 'it clearly matters to you that you came fifth today. Was there a special reason you wanted to do better?' is preferable to, 'But darling, you did really well, so don't get so upset!'

Teachers

* '"That was okay. But if you do it this way next time you might find it easier" is better than an outright complaint because it leaves me feeling okay' *(14)*

59 Don't compare her to others

When our girls are babies, it is natural for all of us to look for similarities between our brand new infant and our partner, any siblings or other relatives so that everyone feels she is part of the family immediately. Not long after, however, the comparisons with others can become far less benign.

Comments such as: 'Your brother would not have dreamt of behaving like that', 'Why can't you be an A student like your sister?' or 'Carrie eats everything when she comes here – why are you so picky?' can be upsetting. Those who lived with such taunts say that, far from being a spur to action, their childhood was tainted by them.

Even handing out equal praise or favourable comparisons can be a hindrance. Saying, 'Jerry's the brainbox and Maria's the family athlete' may give each child something to be proud of but limits the likelihood that either will explore their full talent in the other's special sphere. And comparisons with parents of the 'you take after me' variety can be dangerous, too. You may have been a budding musician and played in local concerts at the same age your daughter is performing, but let it be her achievement unsullied by inheritance. Any girl will want to be herself and not likened to anyone else.

Parents

* each child will respond in her own individual way to a situation because she is unique. Comparisons may stunt her development and undermine her confidence in herself

* make it clear there is room for more than one mathematician, poet, pianist or tennis star in the family

* don't compare your daughter with how you were or what you did at her age. She is herself, not you, and you've probably glamorised the memory!

* labelling makes children resentful and can tempt them to do the opposite out of spite

Teachers

* see each child as an individual, not in the context of her family. Never compare her to a sibling to disparage, coerce or even praise work

* the most useful, and constructive, comparison to make is with her previous best work or performance

* be especially supportive of originality and creativity through which she is exploring and expressing her difference

60 Don't swamp her with your success

Acorns seldom grow under the great oak.

If we want our daughter to be able gradually to recognise when she's done well and be open about her pleasure in her accomplishments rather than rely on us for warm words, we can set an example by describing occasions when things go well for us. However, it is possible for parents to go too far and swamp their daughters with their success and thus overemphasise its value. It is important to leave room for her to feel that small advances are worthwhile and valuable and to avoid implying that each child has to excel to fit in – or suffer derision or rejection.

Where parental success is paraded, it can create an impossible act to follow. Though many daughters follow in their father' or mother's footsteps and are happy to do so, legions of others get put off by the anticipated competition and feel intimidated by any expectation to match their achievement. The best gauge of balance in the matter is whether we suggest we are better as a person for our success and feel superior, which is dangerous. If, on the other hand, we explain it as the result of hard work, luck and embracing opportunity, we are less likely to arouse complex reactions, resentments and fears.

Parents

* handle your own successes with sensitivity. Convey surprise rather than worthiness, and attribute it to your judgement, hard work and good fortune, not genius

* any significant success of yours will be evident; there'll be no need to blow your own horn

* don't strive to excel at everything. Doing something well enough, and sometimes not quite making it, sets a healthier example

* where two parents are successful in different fields, a girl may find it harder to find her own niche. So value her particular strengths, and don't compete with one another, either!

Teachers

* when a girl struggles with a problem of understanding, it won't help her to declare that it is really very simple and then to re-explain it in the same way and at the same speed

* ask if anyone in the class is willing to describe how she made sense of the task or procedure

* underachieving girls will be motivated by the successful efforts of other strugglers, not by the success of the class star

CHAPTER 8

Bribes, Rewards and Incentives

The tactic so many parents resort to in order to nudge their reluctant daughter into action is offering a bribe. That's what most people call them but they are more correctly to be described as inducements, in the form of incentives and rewards. A bribe is something offered to persuade someone to do something illegal or wrong, whereas what we generally offer is an incentive to persuade our child to undertake something legal and desirable – and, usually, in her own interest – that otherwise she would not do. Perhaps we use the term 'bribe' because we feel some guilt about what we're doing because it is seen as a last resort and we would prefer that it was not necessary.

Incentives and rewards can work well but they must be used very carefully, at all ages. When girls are very young, although tactics such as star charts and stickers can help impatient and lively youngsters with short-time horizons see their progress represented visually, the approach can reinforce and internalise the importance of being 'good'. An additional danger is that even five-year-olds can get cheeky and debate how many stars any behaviour deserved, so an approach designed to reduce friction can increase it if introduced without appreciating the extent to which a girl will regain control if she feels manipulated. For example, it can be foolhardy to offer girls a special reward for eating if there are concerns, for this may introduce a further level of interference that may have sparked off the problem initially.

The truth is that we often use incentives to engineer a particular outcome that is our priority. Presenting suggestions and goals in this way may multiply the opportunities to please, but if overused, girls can feel affronted that they are not trusted, reawakening any dormant self-doubt.

Girls are subtle, more manipulative and experienced emotional blackmailers. They may curry favour close to results time to get a bigger reward; they may pester for a reward when the parent had not considered one; they may strop and complain that so and so received something, suggesting that you are mean. If this script sounds familiar, it's time to prepare your defences and reconsider your tactics!

There is no obvious age after which rewards and incentives are best avoided. However, the closer children are to college and working life, the more they need to rely on motivating themselves.

61 Be clear about the purpose

I don't want any money to make me practise my 'cello. If I wanted to do it more often, I'd do it anyway! (12)

Incentives come in various forms and send various messages. There is the 'sweeten the pill' incentive, which we use to show we realise that something is difficult. We might say, 'I can see that you might run out of steam because this is quite a challenge. When you're done, I'll give you something to show I appreciate what you've done.'

There is the 'kick up the butt' incentive that says, in effect, 'I'm not sure you'll do it without something to tempt you.' For example, you might offer her £100 if she manages to reach the age of sixteen without smoking.

There is also the negative or threatening incentive. Instead of offering some prize, the inducement is to avoid experiencing an outright penalty or even simply not receiving something they would otherwise have. A parent might say: 'Unless you improve your marks, I won't pay for your driving lessons like I did your brother' or 'If you don't stop plaguing your sister, I'll take away all your Barbies.'

Parents

* think carefully whether your reasons for offering an incentive are justified or if there is an alternative approach that may be more suitable, such as showing interest in a project and offering to hear a daily progress report

* consider the importance of the particular target or outcome in question. If it marks a crucial turning point or if something very significant hangs on it, there may be more reason to encourage her to do her very best

* ask whether she wants or needs a reward or incentive. She could now be old enough to appreciate the importance of this moment, too, and she may want to meet the challenge without help

Teachers

* think whether any incentive you offer will help her to do her best, or whether it is to raise your overall results and personal ranking

62 Rewards are more effective as surprises

I prefer surprise. It's nice when they've put in time and effort on something. (11)

A reward can be agreed in advance as an incentive, or it can be offered afterwards, produced as a surprise in recognition of our appreciation. Rewards are most helpful and enjoyable if they are not announced in advance, for two reasons. Given in this way, they not only avoid any unpleasant negotiation about whether the suggested reward is big enough but also reduce the chance that any girl will intentionally under perform in order to continue to benefit.

My grandmother, brought up over a century ago, used to warn all of us grandchildren, 'I want doesn't get.' It was a typical Edwardian homily, designed to warn children against covetousness. Surprises aren't dangled beforehand and are therefore more spontaneous and far less open to manipulation by either side.

Parents

* keep it as a genuine surprise. A financial reward that is prised out of you afterwards is not a surprise – unless you are! Praise is a form of reward. We generally reject the practice of double punishment, so why should we be so open to double rewards?

* in order to retain our gesture as a surprise, it follows that we cannot produce rewards too often

* surprises do not have to cost money. But the more toys and goodies children possess, the harder it can be to find simple ways to please them. Examples could include cooking together, letting her use something of yours that she covets or staying up later one weekend

Teachers

* giving surprises to individual students could lay a teacher open to favouritism. However, activities which students enjoy, such as having extra time on the computer, drawing on the board or being asked to run errands during lesson time, can be offered as a surprise reward

* beware rewarding girls who seek to become teacher's pet by acting the goody goody

63 Keep targets manageable: ask, can she realistically deliver?

Girls like to work with adults who have confidence in them and ask them to stretch themselves, because that is when they give of their best and make progress. Doing well when the challenge is easy is neither exciting nor rewarding. But challenges must be set to tempt children to develop themselves, not put them off because they are overambitious and feel threatening. A target set too high is as unhelpful as one set too low.

We know that a target or expectation is realistic when the girl involved agrees that it is achievable. If her view is more pessimistic than ours, she may reject the objective and the reward before she starts: we should never set our child up to fail. If goals appear to her consistently unrealistic the reward will never be earned, which could lead either to a disenchanted and more self-doubting child who then refuses to engage at all, or to a heated argument about how close she got and what other recognition she might deserve given the advance she did achieve.

Parents

* ask her what she thinks she can handle

* help her to devise clear plans to meet her goal

* if she seeks an easier target, start there and work up. Self-belief is so important to longer-term striving that it must be securely in place

* girls often underestimate their ability and do not usually aim low simply to get an easier ride. If she is pessimistic, it could signify a fragile confidence that needs attention

* encourage her to mix short- and longer-term goals

Teachers

* make sure the goal, deadline and expectations are clear

* help girls to assess whether the conditions have been met, and face the consequences if not

* if you detect under-confidence, suggest she prepares a detailed study plan so she realises that it is possible

* don't constantly move the goal posts as this may suggest that achievement was somehow not good enough. Ask whether she's ready for the next challenge or needs some time for everything to settle

64 Reward her with your presence, not presents

Grandma always comes with little gifts for us, but I still prefer grandpa because he takes the time to talk to us and he seems nicer and kinder. (7)

Rewards are used, typically, as a sign that we appreciate what our daughter did and to encourage her. Another good reason for using rewards, when used with care, is that they give children little boosts along the otherwise endless journey that is growing and learning.

Children seem naturally materialistic. Any girl will cotton on very quickly to how much things cost, and they are hawkish as they watch and assess whether a sibling or, especially, a step-sibling gets better gifts than she does. But they are also hard-wired to detect insincerity or superficial gestures, as indicated in the quote above. They know how easy it is for many – though not all – parents to buy something. The best way to show that we truly appreciate her effort is to put some effort into our gesture, which means sharing our scarcest resource: time. As one ten-year-old said, 'I'm one of five so one-to-one time with my mum or dad is special.' Our time with her will genuinely encourage her; will demonstrate genuine appreciation, regard and approval and has infinite, not specific, value.

Parents

* depending on her age, watch her doing something she enjoys, sit with her while she eats, chat as she falls asleep, give her a lift to a friend's or play a game

* quiet time together can be as important as action packed time. Turn off your phone!

* give more generously of your time if there have been any problems or family difficulties recently as she may be unsettled and will almost certainly need you more

* if you're a non-resident parent, after she's had a big success, make a special effort to keep any promise to visit or go out

Teachers

* find a moment to have a special quiet conversation that details her achievement and shows you are interested in and value her as an individual

* show a personal touch by relating the current work to something she wrote previously

* point out what this good piece of work means for her future possibilities and potential

65 Let her help to choose the treat or incentive

I don't get presents. I prefer something I've wanted to do, like an outing or trip to the cinema. (10)

Letting her help to choose the treat or incentive will lessen the possibility that she may see the incentive as a surreptitious attempt by us to control her as it is a celebration on her terms.

If we choose the treat, we have to guess what she would like, and we might get it wrong – missing something either obvious or an as yet undisclosed passion. If she helps to choose the treat, it need not stop it from being a nice surprise. After a pleasing outcome, we can say she deserves a treat and she can help to select it, not forgetting to give some guidance as to the appropriate scale of the cost or event.

During the treat, she can feel like a queen, having special influence and attention for a short while as on a birthday, which will contrast strongly with her daily diet of school when she has to fall into line, be one of a very large crowd and sometimes play second fiddle to friends.

Parents

- the choice of treat will necessarily vary according to a girl's age. It could be a little toy, some sweets or an extra story at bedtime, something that relates to her personal passion or hobby, choosing the destination for a special trip out or a DVD to watch just with you or with the whole family at the weekend or the choice of menu for a celebratory meal at home or out

Teachers

- there is less scope for choice in a classroom context, but rather than determine what the treat should be, if there is some scope for choice it should be offered

66 Money talks . . . back, so take care if you use it!

My brother always asks in advance and his list is so long! (8)

Children often argue about the size of the reward they deserve and push for more. What was intended as a generous gesture can degenerate into a battle of wits and power. 'I'll do it for £10, not for only £5' is a not unfamiliar cry in households where money talks loudly and is used to ensure parental will prevails. Even small children can barter over the appropriate payment, for example, for being good at the dentist.

To negotiate every penny is an obvious way to take control in a situation in which a girl senses financial manipulation. And if money is always accorded value as a reward, it may also become something she could desire strongly – and take – if she ever feels ignored and resentful.

Adolescent girls may be especially prone to cadge from and wheedle their dads. If they associate femininity with flirting and see dads or boys as potential soft touches and game for a challenge, which many girls do, they're more likely to try their dad than their mum who knows the game and will play it back straight.

Parents

* if you hear, 'My friends have all been given £100 for doing well' don't automatically cough up. Her real reward is discovering later that life's best rewards are rarely financial

* lack of money may be a convenient temporary excuse. But when any appears she'll be there, hand held out

* we might give something freely but recipients often ask why

* where money talks, it implies: spending is best; money buys influence; money matters more than time

* when it starts to talk back, a child can say: I'm not bothered or that biddable; I reject your money *and* you!

Teachers

* ask for students' views about the value of money as a reward in class discussion time

* point out that the more money children receive via financial rewards, the less they need: unless the amount rises, the incentive becomes progressively devalued

* reflect on how much you value your job because of or despite the money paid

67 Don't let money become the family's emotional currency

Mum and I had a huge falling out yesterday. She felt so guilty about it she took me out today and bought me a load of new clothes. (17)

No girl should ever feel that the bigger the present or the more money she is given, the more she is loved. Love cannot and should not be measured by price-tags. How much you love a child should never become linked to how much money you are prepared to spend on her. Where effort, commitment and love become closely equated with money and costly gifts, children can ask for ever bigger gifts for proof of love and use emotional blackmail to get them.

Blackmail may occur when gifts are used to fill emotional or time gaps in relationships; when they are purchased either to say sorry or to assuage guilt. Of course all dads and mums like to buy a little gift after a trip away, but if it stops being a surprise and becomes an expectation and lever, we have to take stock. Any complaint on the lines that something more was expected because the trip had been a long one will show it is time to think afresh about how we make up for any time she misses with us.

Parents

* when financial rewards become emotional currency, children can think: 'Prove you're really pleased by giving more', or 'I did it anyway, but hey, let's lay on some guilt and see what happens!'

* stand up for yourself: don't let her exploit your love and ensure she knows, through the little things that you do and say, that you love her without proving it through giving presents

* if you feel guilty about frequent absence, talk to her directly about how sad this makes you and phone her as regularly as you can at an agreed time so she knows she is 'kept in mind'. Presents will then be less necessary

Teachers

* where girls are used to relationships at home that are conditional and based on trading, they may try the same tactics with you. Understand where this might come from and be quiet and firm rather than angry

* remember the theory: the key to safe striving is to ensure that motivation is self-generated, not created by someone else either playing on guilt or applying undue pressure

68 Focus on internal, not external rewards

Where motivation rests upon extrinsic guilt or pressure, there is less sense of self-determination. Howard Hall, Professor of Sport and Exercise Psychology, De Montfort University.

Psychological theory distinguishes between 'intrinsic' and 'extrinsic' rewards. Extrinsic rewards are those that exist outside the child, for example, money, toys, new clothes or perhaps the present of a pet. The Concise Oxford Dictionary defines extrinsic as not belonging to, not essential.

Internal, or intrinsic, rewards, by contrast, belong naturally. They lie inside each of us as positive thoughts and experiences and can be understood as essential. Examples of internal rewards are pride and pleasure; a satisfied curiosity or a sense of mastery and capability; or feeling fit, healthy and agile. Rewards are usually posed to offer encouragement and increase motivation, yet we know the most effective motivation is self-motivation. We all have to learn to do things because we want to, because we enjoy the self-satisfaction that usually flows from effort, progress and achievement. Girls need to learn to acknowledge and value these feelings and consider them sufficient reward.

Parents

* when something goes well, ask her how she feels so she learns to 'read' and acknowledge the internal benefits of making an effort and doing herself justice

* external rewards depend on others; they pale as they become predictable and eventually become mere tokens of success. To remain an effective incentive, they have to increase

* internal rewards, by contrast, are within each person's control. If the pleasure of success fades, she simply raises the target

Teachers

* try to ensure that each girl understands and feels comfortable inside with the mark given or comment made and that she has learned something

* make sure the benefit is doing well, not simply receiving the accolade or bonus points. The older girls get, the more they like to gamble with manipulative games with rewards, and they may get hooked

69 If rewards backfire, drop them

Rewards and incentives may backfire for several reasons. She may refuse to accept them, she may argue endlessly about the nature of the reward, or she may go so far but stop just short of the agreed threshold and still demand the reward. If any tactic is no longer working or has turned sour, how should we respond?

The first action is to stop using rewards altogether, rather than trying to devise another that may work better. The next is to reflect on why this strategy has become problematic. It could be that she wants to show that she doesn't need them. She might be rebelling against being treated like a puppet and want more autonomy and control in her life. It may be that her self-confidence has taken a tumble for some reason so she is now frightened of failing and is no longer trying. It is also quite possible that she has simply got too big for her boots and is just trying it on.

A girl will give of her best when the atmosphere around her is emotionally uncluttered and she feels stimulated by a sense of personal growth, self-discovery and autonomy. She is unlikely to feel in command and free when she feels pushed and pulled by other people's targets and fears emotional rejection if she fails.

Parents

* indicate you are pleased to drop the use of rewards because you prefer to rely on trust

* convey clearly that you are confident she can and will deliver, for her own benefit and future

* if you need to, remind her, firmly, of any agreement and restate that you assume it will be adhered to

* from about the age of ten, invite her to summarise the arguments in favour of working and trying hard and the downside of letting things slip

* she will make the effort when she knows she can say her piece and is respected

Teachers

* rewards systems have to be consistent throughout any school. If the system does not seem to work with individual students, think more deeply about the possible explanation. Consider the experience of colleagues and brainstorm potentially more effective and flexible approaches, such as making specific tasks easier (fewer spellings to learn) or a quiet place to do homework in school with you or a colleague present to help her concentrate

* it is through having responsibility that children find out about themselves. Put her in charge of as much of her learning and assessment as possible and give her jobs around the class or school

70 Channel competition safely

The competitive instinct can lead to shallow growth and the Brownie badge collecting mentality. Tony Gardiner, Professor of Mathematics, Birmingham University.

Girls compete in different ways and over different things. For example, they attach a great deal of importance to how they look, and believe that having fashionable clothes and a slim figure as well as brains will help to make them popular – the ultimate prize.

Research shows that where either parents or teachers set up competitions to raise performance, the outcome is often an anxious child. If a child feels that status and approval hang on a test result she is more likely either to experience pre-test nerves and debilitating panic or to become depressed later if she is disappointed by the result. The more parents encourage competition and demand top results, the more a girl could be tempted to cheat or impede others to secure that advantage and approval.

Parents

* it is better to identify a specific goal – 'Try to improve on your chemistry lab work' – than a general one: 'Go for an A this time'

* don't fuel competition between brothers and sisters. Each child needs to be successful in her own way, and accepted unconditionally for who she is

* fun competitions are fine. 'See if you can beat me to the top of the stairs' is a great way to get her on the way to bed

Teachers

* research shows that when competition is a main teaching tool, children become anxious

* encourage children to perform to improve, not impress, and give them feedback so they can see any progress made

* the use of cooperative rather than competitive games can show how much fun can be gained from simply joining in and exercising one's wits

CHAPTER 9

Using Praise to Encourage Learning and Behaviour

It would not be surprising if many readers turned to this chapter first. People often seek guidance when they feel things are going off-track. In terms of what presents a problem to parents, school performance and behaviour are the two big ones. Praise, encouragement and positive feedback are especially valuable and effective in these two areas, and far more likely to produce happier and more self-directed children than punishment, harsh criticism or humiliation. They are also the areas in which parents can find themselves in difficulty, despite using a range of 'positive' and apparently recommended inducements, without really understanding why. It is for this reason that learning and behaviour are addressed at this point in the book for it is important that the general principles of effective praise and some of the pitfalls of effusive praise are absorbed before seeking answers to any immediate problem. It is important to be clear about the best ways to get the best from our children, especially when they are trying to gulp down the fresh air of freedom.

But first, a few words about both discipline and learning. The better these are understood, the easier it will be to keep feedback and attention positive and constructive. Learning is an emotional activity and a very complex process. It involves far more than a child simply opening her mind and receiving the knowledge being presented by the teacher, because her state of mind – how she feels and interprets the world around her – inevitably influences her willingness and capacity to absorb information. When children struggle at school there are frequently quite complex explanations. Difficult life events, including bullying, can distress, distract and preoccupy children so they are unable to concentrate. These same events may threaten children's self-belief because they often introduce uncertainty and powerlessness, which make children less willing to take the risks that learning entails. Panic freezes the mind and if we expect information to be over our heads it can appear jumbled and confusing. Learning and striving can arouse a range of fears: fear of incompetence, fear of failure, fear of reprimand and fear of ridicule. Ultimately, children are agents of their own learning. Rather than be forced to absorb some information and then receive the 'gift' or reward of positive feedback (many people's view of how to improve results) it is better that a girl be offered scope to decide *how* best she learns, *when* she is ready to try harder or *whether* she needs incentives or tokens of appreciation.

Approaches to discipline should also encourage self-discipline and autonomy. Girls should not be forced to comply with adult rules and wishes in every sphere of their life beyond a certain age. Challenging behaviour needs to be understood more than punished. Early on, of course, it is important to set your daughter clear guidelines to keep her safe and to create calm and predictability so she can feel secure; but as she grows older she must then be encouraged to make choices, judge situations for herself and assess the consequences. Eventually, by her late teens, she should develop her own priorities and values and manage her own study patterns, time and behaviour. Those with a duty of care will encourage this if they value and reward reflection and responsibility and treat compliance more as an expectation.

71 Success is always relative

I had a greater sense of achievement from finishing 73rd in the national school championships aged fourteen than from coming sixth in the 10,000 metres in the 1972 Olympics which I was expected to win. It was a disaster for me. But I tried to hang on to the positive view that I was sixth best in the world. David Bedford, former 10,000m World Record Holder and now Race Director of the London Marathon.

It is important to realise that what might be a small, unremarkable step forward for one girl can be a significant mark of progress for another, and a successful result for someone who needs to work hard to do well may be a disappointing one for someone else who rides challenges easily and is capable of better. No one should be denied her parents' pleasure just because someone with greater talent was in the line-up to outshine her personal effort.

In school, children are viewed as learners and are judged and differentiated by academic ability. At home we must see our daughter in the round and as multi-talented; always offer a sense of hope and help her develop the self-respect necessary to acquire a positive self-image even if academic excellence is not her strong point.

Parents

* every girl learns and develops in a different way and takes a different amount of time. 'She's a late developer' may be the truth, rather than a convenient, embarrassed cover up response to sceptical friends or relatives

* remember that stressful experiences can put learning on hold; and everyone needs times when they tread water rather than surge forward

* ask her whether it felt good to her. If it did and she's not pretending, that's good enough

* if your friends' children are apparently doing better than yours, avoid feeling competitive. Yours are still loveable as they are

Teachers

* consider each piece of work as a good or less good one *for each student at this moment,* not in relation to the standard you ultimately expect

* whole class praise is good from time to time so everyone feels the benefit

72 Match the applause to the achievement

Oh good job, Sunita! I love how you are sitting quietly at the table! Everyone, put your hands together for a little clap!

'Say it enthusiastically' is a mantra adopted by many parenting and management gurus and therefore by parents. Of course, it is undoubtedly better to sound pleased than to describe pleasure with a deadpan expression and flat voice; however, the fervour espoused by many can go too far in the other direction and not only sound fake but also create too much tension around the requirement to continue to deserve the accolades.

If praise is about appreciation, and appreciation involves estimating the worth of something, we need to match the applause to the achievement.

Parents

* encouragement includes waiting quietly and patiently while a child works out how to do something. It shows trust that she'll manage

* saying something's great before it has been achieved is false and can imply there is pressure to get it right. However, showing appreciation of endeavour thus far suggests that that is good enough

* children feel pride and pleasure, not when they receive phoney feedback about their brilliance, but when they know they worked hard and have something significant to show for it

Teachers

* ask a student how she would like a good piece of work acknowledged other than with your written comment, if at all

* accumulate small achievements to justify a bigger splash of recognition. Three in one week or in one term could earn different rewards

* for young girls, a week, or even a day, is long enough. Older girls can relate to improvements over a longer period

73 Praise girls' passion and purpose

A UNESCO report, *International Commission on Education for the Twenty-first Century*, published in 1996, identified four kinds of learning: learning to know; learning to live together; learning to be; and learning to do.

It is what girls know, or rather seem not to know, that upsets parents most. Yet learning also entails finding out about oneself: discovering personal passions, personal styles and a sense of purpose – the 'learning to do and be' featured in the extract above. These will take any girl further in life than dutiful delivery. Initiative is to be supported, even if at the start mistakes are made. Instead of gasping with frustration or outrage at the risk taken, it can be commended. Focus, instead, on whether sensible preparations were made to deal with any possible dangers or difficulties.

Occasionally, a daughter's passion and purpose will lead her into lies and wrongdoing: she may claim she went somewhere different; she may spend money on something she agreed not to or listen to friends rather than you. Understand that she could be struggling with competing demands and lures (though these must be legal) not being defiant.

Parents

* having opportunities to work with friends, even if they gossip and seem to be 'off task' some of the time, can benefit learning through enhancing language, social and communication skills

* learning is inevitably a social activity. It never happens in a vacuum. It always involves listening, interacting with a teacher, responding to peer and teachers' expectations and 'self' assumptions that are so often clarified in reference to others. Social confidence can encourage more confident work

Teachers

* if you have class awards, don't forget to acknowledge humour or other social attributes

* encourage girls to feel comfortable in group-based projects in which they take the lead and share their ideas

* find out what individual girls feel passionate about and enable them to give presentations about these

* 'groupthink' is greater than the sum of its parts. Demonstrate through an exercise that ideas can deepen and strengthen when people work together

74 Let the teacher do the teaching

Parents always expect higher than you do. When you're pleased with something, they always find something wrong with it. It's very upsetting. (11)

When young children are proud of something they have done, of course they want to show it to us. Rather than burst their bubble of confidence with critical comments, we should aim to appreciate the piece of work and accept that they are pleased with it. If we spot something wrong or something we felt could have been done better – as we're almost bound to, being adult – we have to think carefully about how and whether to say anything. It is, essentially, for the teacher, who knows the standard expected for our child's age, to do the teaching.

If she asks us to check it over, we can be more straightforward, but always having first commented positively on something we liked about the work and having checked she is ready to hear any suggestions for changes. Some children will be happy to get stuck back in; others may decide they will leave it as it is, nonetheless, and this is their choice.

Parents

* get too critical and she won't let you near to help at all

* avoid changing anything or adding finishing touches as she'll no longer see it as her work

* only the teacher can know what to expect from a girl of her age, what is really being tested in the homework, or what's best for her to learn next

* if there is a big difference between what she produces at home and in class, consult rather than berate the teacher. The problem could be a talkative friend, boredom, disruptive classmates or feeling different if she does her best

Teachers

* parents who complain are parents that care. Go easy on them and try not to take it personally

* guidance for parents on helping with homework issued at the start of the academic year may help to keep the ground clear

75 Every day can't be judgement day

I don't like my mum coming to watch me play in matches. One time recently she said, 'You could have played better', yet we won 13:1 so what more did she want? (11)

If our bosses were to check us over each day and give us daily marks out of ten, we'd end up ragged and neurotic. That's how children must feel when they are regaled with constant expressions of pleasure and disapproval. They will find it hard to find that all-important necessary private space when they feel watched continuously. Boys tend to grab the private time they need quite openly. Girls are more surreptitious and secretive and will carve it out in more dangerous ways, through not eating or lying or keeping information back. If parents are too inquisitive and judgemental about each day's events and efforts, a child may decide to give nothing away at all and either clam up or tell a load of manufactured stories.

Parents

* encouragement contains no judgement: it leaves her free to take herself forward in her own way

* use encouraging comments to help her to feel you're appreciating rather than judging:
– you've put so much effort into that!
– I wish I'd done such interesting things at school
– it's hard for you but you will crack it

* take away any guilt or shame she might feel if she anticipates judgement: 'That wasn't at all like you. Let's put it behind us and start again tomorrow'

Teachers

* make earning any 'good work' stickers fun

76 Show interest but don't be intrusive

In some ways, I'd prefer my mum to understand more about what I do in my sport. But I also like it that she doesn't breathe down my neck. I have space and it's my thing. (10)

One mum who had a very high-powered job said she was not going to attend the parent consultation session at her daughter's school because she considered it up to them to get the teaching right. She wasn't interested to hear what she could do – that was what she was paying them for.

How wrong she was! Of course we should be interested in our child's progress and happiness in all areas of development at school. For all schoolchildren, school is almost as important as their family; for older children, it is probably more important.

But we have a dilemma. After the age of eight or so children relish school as the place where they can be themselves and get up to a little mischief away from the often intense gaze of their parents' constant scrutiny. They need some privacy. Their need for praise from us becomes offset gradually by their need for autonomy. When girls want our appreciation, they'll tell us all we need to know.

Parents

* ask open-ended questions that allow her to withhold detail. 'Did anything good or bad happen today?' not 'Who did you play with and what happened?' And start by talking about *your* day

* ask casually about marks gained. 'That tricky maths sheet, how did it go down?' rather than 'What mark did you get, will I be pleased?'

* if you overhear talk of a difficulty, offer to discuss it but don't demand details

* make sure questions are genuine, not designed to find out something else

* take an interest in her work but don't take it over and do it for her

Teachers

* show interest in her personal passions or hobbies but step back if she seems uncomfortable about it

* her family experiences influence a great deal. It is important to understand and acknowledge these but also to treat anything you learn with respect as many children prefer this information to remain private

* at parent-teacher events and in newsletters, stress the important role that parents can play in encouraging schoolwork and being interested in any developments at the school

77 Give her hope

The horrendous danger in our A-grade obsession is that we are imposing labels on plants that are still growing. Dr Martin Stephen, High Master of St Paul's Boys' School.

Getting there is as important as arriving and along the road there should always be hope. Girls give up either because they have been told over and over again that they are a hopeless case or because they doubt their capacity to do well for other reasons. The message many hear is demoralising and undermining: 'You won't if you don't . . .'; 'You will never if you carry on . . .' or 'You're a born loser, never been any success with . . .' Rather than risk further failure and have salt rubbed in already torn egos, many will decide not to try. Labels tend to stick and act as straightjackets, which will make it difficult for her to escape the destiny she hears described.

Girls need to hear far more upbeat and hopeful messages that will not only boost their self-belief but also make any target seem manageable and easy to keep up once achieved. 'Of course this is hard, but just take it one step at a time and you'll have no problem'; 'You've managed to stay close and not run off from the vegetable section all the way to the meat. It's not so far now to the checkout. Did you think you think it would be this easy? I knew you could do it!' for example.

Parents

* remind her of past successes so she can think positively and believe in herself

* if success appears unfamiliar or scary and seems to carry heavy responsibilities for continuing in the same vein, it may be easier for a girl to remain the devil she knows

* if she sets herself a goal that she's failed to complete before, don't remind her of the past failure. Greet each resolution as a first and stay positive

* motivation is grounded in hope and experience

Teachers

* sarcasm and ridicule usually puncture hope. Don't use them

* make sure that her hope is grounded in a practical reality – help her to put together a plan

* break the challenge down into small, manageable chunks and remind her of difficulties she has previously overcome

* never say what one teacher said to a mother: 'Your daughter is destined for a life of failure if she continues like this'

78 Encourage her to make links and connections

Creative thinking expands children's horizons and is fun, because it produces surprises. It encourages girls to see new ways of doing things and to solve problems, which should enable them to feel more confident and capable. Parents and teachers can mitigate girls' tendency to play safe and avoid intellectual adventure by making it a familiar family or classroom practice to find and enjoy unusual links between ideas, events and products or between one topic area and another. Of course, it is also important to go easy on the criticism.

Many people believe that children start out more creative and resourceful because they have not become locked into set ways of seeing things through the pressure to conform, the desire to please or the constraints of logic. It is a shame to see the spirit and individuality of a child diminish when she has to fit the formality of an organised classroom; but it will not get irretrievably lost if we avoid over-emphasising the benefit of being 'good' and applaud her imagination and ability to see links. If something goes wrong, such as a cake sinking in the middle or a clay pot collapsing, better to laugh and liken it to something else altogether than focus on the 'failure'.

Parents

* cartoonists exploit unusual connections and generate humour from the unexpected. Collect cartoons from newspapers and magazines in a scrapbook and laugh at them together

* encourage making connections from an early age. Make events trigger familiar songs or stories; say, 'Now that reminds me of when . . .'

* number links can be made by comparing the dots and symbols on dice, playing cards and dominoes

* play word association and alphabet games when you walk and travel

* don't get upset by mess when she is creating or experimenting

Teachers

* be understanding of work that's not quite what you had in mind, provided it is thought through and demonstrates understanding. The student could be a future Nobel prize winner!

* avoid commanding total obedience in every way. Allow girls to joke about funny things that come to their minds, even if this verges on being cheeky

* girls who are naturally timid and like to be told exactly what to do should be encouraged to experiment, and those who enjoy experimentation need sometimes to stick to what's expected

79 Two steps forward, one back

Learning anything is a strange business for it rarely happens in a predictable way or to a set pattern. Children learn, mature and develop in phases and spurts and each one will manage it in her unique way. Girls get 'eureka' moments when everything falls into place but then they can get quite scared and may want to return to the time they were more dependent and needed to rely on help. That way, they don't risk being wrong. At each stage of advance, they can feel quite exposed. Learning, therefore, is often a case of two steps forward, one step back as the knowledge or new behaviour gets to feel normal.

In relation to behaviour, girls often need to test parental reactions after they have been accommodating for a while, to check if their parents really have become cooler and kinder and won't revert to being harsh if she slips up again. If parents ride the highs and lows because this is understood, this is a form of acceptance and affirmation that has the same effect as giving direct praise.

We may also witness 'two steps back, three great leaps forward'. Younger children can appear to go into reverse before they make a significant developmental advance – their brains seem to take a holiday before they then go full speed ahead.

Parents

* when a girl needs to tread water for a while and take time out from the pressure of eternal 'progress', she should certainly not be frowned upon or punished

* if your daughter seems to have 'lost it' and become confused or cannot do something she could before, wait patiently. Within a week it is likely she will have rediscovered the ability, taken a leap forward – or she will have become poorly and have to stay in bed!

* children learn by doing but they also learn by sleeping on it, imagining it, 'playing with' the idea and thinking it through subconsciously. Don't ask for minute evidence of step-by-step learning

Teachers

* targets, assessment tests and league tables assume that every child is developing as the 'average' when each one progresses uniquely

* try to include some flexibility in the study programme

* give a girl who is flagging evidence that she is not stupid, merely working on the problem in her way and at her own speed

* try to convince her that she'll catch up, and impress that, like any investment, past performance is no guarantee of future outcomes!

80 Pick on one thing at a time

When parents reach the end of their tether because everything a child does seems to make life difficult, the temptation is to complain about everything at once and tackle all the issues in one offensive. This can be the worst response because it rarely works and leaves a child despondent and confused.

It is hard for any young child to hold lots of rules and expectations in their heads at once. It is also likely that constant nagging and criticism will be seen as a sign by self-doubting girls that she is no good because she's unable to please. As has been said, until a child has a strong and separate sense of self, she is not able to be convinced that a complaint about how she has behaved is not a complaint directed at her as a person.

Everyone benefits by picking one aspect of behaviour to turn around at a time. The chances of success are higher, the nagging and edginess reduces and life is more generally relaxed. Most valuable, once things have improved on the central problem, other challenging behaviour tends to disappear as a result of fewer fights, less resentment and a higher profile of praise and encouragement.

Parents

* don't pile on the demands or the complaints; this can cause tempers to flare

* identify the behaviour that bothers you most or the time of day that is most trying and start there. Drop the nagging about other problems until the top priority is sorted out

* let her know that this is your plan, and make it seem like a fair contract: she does her bit and you do yours, which is staying cool about other matters

* for schoolwork, suggest that she works to improve one subject at a time. Don't ask her to pull out the stops on her reading and her maths, or her science and her history at the same time

Teachers

* with a challenging class, reflect upon the source of the main problem – a handful of particularly disruptive students, classroom management (because they sit and disrupt together) or teaching style (because some seem to lose interest very quickly). Pick on the most plausible explanation and unravel that problem first

* give girls who struggle clear and achievable short-term goals so they know exactly where they must focus and see the way forward. When one does well, make sure she knows and accepts that it was her knowledge and understanding that got her there, not fluke

CHAPTER 10

Avoiding the Perils of Perfectionism

Many people have become concerned that an increasing pressure to achieve and do well has led to more high-flying students becoming perfectionists and 'success junkies', dependent on their regular fix of achievement and accolade, success and celebration, without which they feel incomplete. For example, in America, the former Dean of Harvard undergraduate college, Harry Lewis, was openly concerned by some students' need to impress and to receive acknowledgement and rewards for everything when he wrote to students, 'You may balance your life better if you participate in some activities purely for fun . . . many of the most important and rewarding things that you do will be recorded on no piece of paper but only as imprints on your mind and soul.'

There are similar concerns in the United Kingdom over the growing pressures in competitive elite sport and the demand for perpetual progress at school. While some children seem able to survive, even thrive on, the pressures, others may develop an unhealthy level of perfectionism that conceals considerable self-doubt and distress because they pursue sometimes impossible goals and are never satisfied with the result. Girls seem particularly prone, and sometimes respond by developing an eating disorder or self-harming, but boys succumb, too.

What attitudes and support help to keep children free from turmoil and competitive anxiety? Research shows that children who aim high, do well, and can sustain success in a healthy and balanced way, work to their own, realistic and flexible, standards and expectations. They can take on board mistakes and failure. They tend to be well-organised, have uncritical parents and strive for their own benefit because they enjoy the activity. They are in control. Most important, they have a robust and stable self-esteem that doesn't rely on proving themselves to others or coming top to buoy them up.

The seeds of unhealthy perfectionism take root where, in the eyes of the child, approval appears conditional on success; where children strive to meet very high and inflexible expectations they see others hold for them; where adults take the credit for, or 'steal' any success; where no success ever seems good enough because targets always shift; where constant challenge generates constant doubt about ability; and where success is lauded, failure is shunned and fear of failure is intense. So perfectionist attitudes do not help children to be happy, despite the often impressive achievements that accumulate: one setback will suggest a future strewn with failure.

81 Keep all goals realistic and flexible

Everyone gets scars on the way to the stars. The title of a song written by Fran Landesman, jazz singer.

Parents and teachers are often tempted to ask a child to go that extra mile and are loathe to make the target easier if the child then struggles. If a problem appears, it tends to be interpreted as attitude and application, not an unrealistic target.

Research shows that being able to be flexible and to compromise on standards and targets is one of the keys to healthy striving. If a girl begins to set tough targets and beats herself up emotionally if she doesn't quite get there, encourage her to go easy. Of course it's great if she does very well but it is more important that she doesn't find herself in the stranglehold of a perfectionist straightjacket.

Parents

* never berate a girl for having not quite excelled, even as a joke

* if she is short-listed for a further test after a preliminary stage, mark that with an interim treat. Don't necessarily wait until the final outcome, as getting that far is creditable

* how perfectionist are you? Try to demonstrate flexibility in your own goal-setting

* don't harbour inflexible goals for your daughter

Teachers

* a girl who frequently misses deadlines may be trying to perform at too high a standard to prove something. Discuss with colleagues how best to readjust her standards and encourage her to be content with work achieved in less time

* make it clear that each student achieves at a different level, and that high performance should not come at the expense of enriching leisure time or mental composure

82 Don't make approval conditional on her success

When my daughter was not selected to be head of her school, I felt let down and almost angry. I got really picky with her. I found myself putting her down. I'm an intelligent and successful businessman and was both horrified and ashamed that I felt this way. It just happened.

At least he admitted his feelings. This father's first reaction – of vindictive disappointment – is more common than anyone would care to accept, although his subsequent insight is far less usual. If we expect good things, it is very easy to feel disappointed and let down if they do not happen, but no child should suffer the burden of believing that success is the only way to maintain either parent's love or approval.

We might have a similar reaction if our daughter behaved badly on an occasion that mattered to us and we felt shown up. If we 'went cold' on her but did not actually reprimand her for a specific wrongdoing, we could be falling into the trap of reserving our approval for times when she makes us feel good.

Parents

* accept that it is not good for her to be perfect, and that every experience, including every setback, is an important stepping stone in learning and growing

* see the funny side and the alternative potential of any shortfalls

* if you find yourself being disappointed by a second best outcome, remind yourself that you are not her and she is not you. In your mind, draw a boundary between you and her and resolve to stop living parasitically through her

Teachers

* treat all students fairly, without favouritism. Accept each one as a worthwhile individual; don't reserve your enthusiasm for the accommodating and successful ones

* show that you value a wide range of attitudes, specialist knowledge and skills. Refer to past achievements and anticipate future ones

* focus on the process as well as the outcome. How the improvement was achieved is the aspect to highlight, rather than the success itself

* encourage all students to take important decisions and responsibility for these, so each one feels trusted by you

83 Let your daughter take, and keep, ownership of the success

Children need to keep possession of any success and realise that it's theirs. No one should run off and tell the world, like it was their achievement and their prize. Head teacher and special educational needs expert.

Of course, our daughter owns her success but it is very easy to take it over and thereby take it from her. That is what we are doing when we use it to make us feel successful. We feel so thrilled by the achievement we are almost driven to run off with it and show it to all our friends by telling them. We can get enormous kudos from our children doing very well in their various activities.

But if we effectively steal her success and spread around any special news, rather than feel fulfilled, our daughter could be left feeling empty and bereft. She could then feel driven to replenish the success, over and over again.

Parents

* personal success should be seen as the child's property, not the parent's. You would not consider borrowing anything of hers without asking, and the same courtesy should apply here

* check first whether she wishes anyone else to know, and if she would like to tell any particular people herself

* asking her not only shows you respect her and her wishes, but also makes the success unambiguously hers

* devaluing something that she believes to be a success also 'steals' the achievement and pleasure from her: 'But a third of the class got that mark. That's not so special!'

Teachers

* when schools use children's achievements to pump up their prospectuses, there is a danger that students will feel used

84 Stay in touch with her reality

Don't be arrogant enough to assume you always know what she wants and how she feels. It is important to keep talking and giving her the opportunity to discuss her fears and feelings freely with you, including those that could hurt or disappoint you.

She must be free to talk about shame, letting you down, always having hankered after some other activity than the one you encouraged or her fear of failure and perhaps distorted imaginings. There will be pluses to discuss, too: which aspects of her life give her the most pleasure, how she rates each of her talents or particular skills.

For example, if you celebrate a child's success, the event should suit her, not us. A ten-year-old could find it hard to relate to a horde of neighbours or relatives descending, talking to each other and enjoying alcohol. She may enjoy adult company, but she may prefer to be alone or with friends her age. If that's the case, of what benefit was the gathering to her?

Parents

* plan the celebration at her level, not at how you would mark some notable feat of yours

* take her worries seriously. Don't ignore something that saddens or annoys her

* if you refuse to see things her way and impose your view, she could lose touch with herself and become your reflection

* younger children make sense of things in surprising ways and readily believe the unbelievable, such as Father Christmas and tooth fairies. Just because you know why something has to be, it does not follow she also understands why

Teachers

* try to uncover any worries that lie behind late, 'lost' or very poor work. There could be distress at home or she could fear demonstrating her total lack of understanding so not bother at all

* appreciate that strong parental antagonism to school and study could dilute a girl's commitment to work. It is a conflicting reality for her and she's likely to struggle with the conflict

85 Talk about 'development', not 'improvement'

Girls who have the opportunity to discover new interests, talents and skills learn more about themselves and establish a pattern of self-discovery that can enrich the rest of their lives. Self-discovery is, indeed, the main purpose: only if they explore what is there inside can they discover their true potential and experience the thrill and excitement that lies in store. The process should be one of self-development, not self-improvement.

Improvement implies that a girl is progressively better and cleverer than how she was before. It suggests that how she was before was not 'right'; yet, to repeat, she needs to see her past as an acceptable part of her. The subtle message could be that she needs to go on getting better and improving herself, trying one new thing after another in order to remain acceptable. We should not demand that she 'fulfil her potential', because we can never know what potential is there or when it is fulfilled. Better to ask her to unpeel a layer or two of possible resistance to reveal her reserve of capability – for her own enjoyment.

Parents

* make it clear that it is the results or the technique that is improving, not her personality or 'self'

* talk about discovery, rather than improvement. 'You're discovering all sorts of new things about yourself!', 'You're discovering you can feel comfortable with maths after all', 'Did you think you could pull out those extra stops and improve your sprint time so successfully?'

Teachers

* separate the girl from the improvement. Refer to her understanding deepening, her application becoming more effective, to her new inspiration or her growing skill at identifying reference materials or with a technique, rather than marvelling at her generalised 'improvement'

86 Don't be wowed by neatness

There is a pattern. The girls who develop eating disorders are such perfectionists. Their handwriting is so neat and their work presented beautifully. They are always the 'good', caring girls. A secondary school counsellor.

Work that is neat and well-presented might seem to suggest that the student is on top of things, thinking carefully, not rushing and taking pride in her work, but it could be a mistake to see the perfect presentation as a sign that all's well – for it might not be.

Neatness can be contrived as a diversion from content, with a girl believing the words alone to be not quite good enough; it can be used as a tactic to impress both the teacher and fellow students, to make her work look perfect as well as being pleasing in itself – the make-up and lipstick applied lovingly to the assignment – just as she may strive to look perfect.

Of course, neatness can imply simply that a student has a natural orderly approach to work that may be time-consuming not time-saving, so it may not conceal deeper doubts; but if a girl is taking so long over work that playtime gets lost and bedtime gets delayed, better not to praise the presentation but to encourage her to use her time more sensibly.

Parents

* focus on the content, not on the presentation and encourage her to appraise it. Ask, 'But what do you think of it? You're the best judge of what you've written'

* try to encourage her to be specific: 'You said you did badly. What was it you thought didn't go right?' or, 'Yes, I liked what you did, but what pleased you in particular?'

* such details help you to assess the accuracy or health of her judgement

* help her to risk not getting full marks by saying you don't need her to prove her ability to you

Teachers

* invite students to moderate each other's work, having first discussed which points, skills and understandings needed to be covered. The judgement any girl applies to another's work will be fresh to apply to her own. The value of presentation should also be assessed

* if you consider someone's neatness could be approaching an obsession, make it clear you like to see words crossed out and don't like headings underlined in different colours and might mark her down if she persists

87 Don't constantly move the goal posts

I'd done very well in school, and outside in music, dance, swimming and so on. I'd loved doing those things, but I was conscious they'd all been organised by my parents. I felt I was having to live up to the expectations other people had of me. I had the sense of being misunderstood, and therefore out of control. I had a double life, my successful public persona and my inside person, who was not very happy and not sure what she really wanted.

Demanding schools and parents are prone to move the goal posts. As soon as one target is in sight and therefore appears easy, another more challenging one is presented to prevent any flagging of effort. Or as soon as one goal has been reached, another is put in place to maintain the momentum: 'If you can achieve that, then surely this is also within reach!' A common example of this process is musical instrument examinations, where having prepared for and sat one grade, another one is immediately presented as the new goal.

But even a successful girl who coasts through challenges should take breaks from constant achievement and have a greater degree of control over her life and commitments. If she says, 'No, that's enough', that is healthy and her wishes should be respected.

Parents

* challenges must tempt girls to discover themselves, not threaten them, put them off or make them feel inadequate until they fulfil them

* when girls are allowed to select the moment to renew their efforts, their readiness reflects their confidence

* shifting goal posts represent a broken deal. They can store up resentment, self-doubt and anxiety

Teachers

* factor in the child's view of what she can, and wants to, achieve and put her in control as far as is practical to reduce the pressure

* asking for perfect answers and work before moving someone on encourages perfectionist attitudes or boredom

88 Accept good enough success

Growing up feeling my best wasn't good enough encouraged me to become defiant and stop trying. But although I appeared no longer to care I continued to beat myself up inside for being useless.

Any girl faced with successive mirage-style targets – ones that disappear as you approach, like the shimmering 'puddles' of water on hot roads on sunny days – will very likely conclude that no success is good enough. If no success, however great, is good enough, a child will never know if she is good enough; or, indeed, if she is any good at all. This is a very uncomfortable thought, so she will need to achieve more success to convince her that she is good enough and worthy of praise. Success, if sought for this reason, will not raise self-esteem or self-belief, or deepen the self-concept. At worst, it deepens self-doubt; at best it leaves someone's self-esteem vulnerable and prone to fluctuation.

Self-belief does not come from a sense that we are perfect but from the knowledge that we are good enough but have more to give.

Parents

* lead her when she's ready. For success to benefit self-worth, a girl needs time to absorb the achievement, be sure she can repeat it and make it part of her identity. Only she can know when she is ready

* being pushed to move on too soon generates considerable anxiety, a noted characteristic of perfectionists who feel driven by others

* good enough success is not a cop out, accepting second best or laziness. It is the result of honest (though perhaps not top notch) striving that produces real progress, and is the guard against either internal or external pressure

Teachers

* let all success be good enough, at least for a time, including your own

* ask your students when they are ready to make an extra push to raise their results or enter a competition

* untidy work can be considered good enough if the content is sound. Find out why the work was apparently rushed; if it was to create time to fit in other valuable activities, it could be a sensible trade-off

89 Taking reasonable risks is important

Mother: *Do up your shoelaces! You might trip and fall over.*
Daughter: *What's the matter? Can't you take a risk? (10)*

This episode shows how easy it is to convey in small ways that taking risks is not a good idea. This girl's response was unusual, for girls are often more risk averse than boys. They don't like to be told off and they like to play by the rules most of the time and not leave too much to chance, preferring to over-prepare than skimp on study. Some develop an attitude described as 'learned helplessness', where they claim incompetence and court as much help and guidance as they can elicit to reduce the risk of getting something wrong.

The ability to take risks is important, for learning is a risky business. Coming down hard when she's risked something and misjudged it could lead her to avoid larger risks. Girls with perfectionist tendencies have very high standards. Fear of falling short tempts some to self-handicap to avoid the anxiety, consciously or unconsciously. She may put things off until it is too late, aim ridiculously high to ensure failure or too low. She may destroy her work; she may even cheat to ensure the outcome. Some develop inexplicable lethargy, pains or eating disorders, any of which provides an excuse to exit the rat race.

Parents

* talk honestly about any mistakes you might have made in the past and any you make now. Let her see that risks often pay off and there's always something to learn if they don't

* encourage her to face her fears, not run from them

* adventurous play that incorporates a measure of planned physical risk or that confronts the unexpected is helpful

* promote self-direction. Don't solve every problem for her and become over-protective

Teachers

* if you make a mistake, be open and honest about it

* raise class awareness of differing attitudes to mistakes by initiating a discussion. Observe any gender patterns, and talk about this

* girls are often more timid and don't relish competitive games. Invite students to reflect upon what winning, losing or participating means to them

* girls with low self-belief have neither the courage to take chances nor the confidence to change. Strive to strengthen self-belief

90 Don't ignore or punish failure

If they only tell you good things, you don't get the true bit. (11)

Parents are often advised to encourage children by ignoring mistakes and focusing on what they do well. This helps girls when they are very young, when they find it hard to control either their bodies or feelings, take the first steps in learning and are too young to live within wall-to-wall rules. However, as they mature they should be honest about the quality and effect of their work and behaviour. But girls tend to take criticism to heart, so mistakes must be discussed extremely carefully. If parents continue to disregard failures while celebrating successes, the hidden message can be that failure is shameful and must be avoided. This view is certainly typical of perfectionists.

Failure is not something to be shunned or punished. It provides factual and neutral information on what went wrong, what has not been understood fully and on what needs to be changed to get it right. The experience of failure becomes shameful where a child has invested her self-worth in doing well, or where a parent relies on a daughter's success for personal satisfaction and happiness, so failure becomes associated with disappointment and discomfort.

Parents

* respond sensitively to setbacks. If her failures become your personal shame, or if her successes lift you from gloom, you make it harder for her

* help her to see where the problem lies: she hadn't understood something, because she rushed at it or because the subject is not her forte. Perhaps she has over-ambitious standards. The problem is *not* that *she* is useless. Make her move beyond self-flagellation

* see failure as neutral. It is not appropriate to rub her nose in it or tease her

* making mistakes can show she is working at the frontier of her knowledge and understanding, so be tolerant

Teachers

* if any girl tries to hide a disappointing result or cries if she gets less than full marks or fails to make the top three, ask to speak to her parents to discuss what might lie behind her self-criticism

* failure can be seen to undermine a girl's mission to be 'good' and please significant others. Help to take the shame out of any failure and clarify the lessons to be learned

* hear her side of the story

CHAPTER 11

Praise and You

Having spoken to countless adults over the years, to people who have been successful as well as those leading less remarkable lives, it is surprising how many were quick to volunteer that their parents, and particularly fathers, never praised them. They never felt their efforts were appreciated and were left with a feeling that they were simply not good enough or not sufficiently interesting personalities to be noticed. For some it has influenced the course of their life, for they are still trying to please, even though the parent is no longer around to watch the show. It remains unfinished business; and while this urge may lead to higher achievement than a more contented childhood might have delivered, the success masks an eternal sadness, sense of being let down and an underlying restlessness.

One acquaintance, who has a high public profile, agreed that her desire to prove herself as good as her brothers in the eyes of her father had generated her need to do well and make a mark from a young age. One man who sits at the top of his profession readily acknowledged the importance of self-esteem and said he had suffered quietly all his life because his father had neither praised him nor appeared to recognise or value his talents. As a consequence, he was happy now to be able to work with young students and graduates to encourage them to strengthen their sense of self through acquiring wider experiences of which they could feel proud.

Someone who experienced difficulty at the other end of the range of parental behaviour is a young woman who showed early musical talent and was expected to meet demanding practice and performance schedules as a result to make it her career. She was praised, but grudgingly and with conditions attached. Her success was never good enough. She felt increasingly that her life was not her own and the only way to regain control was to give up. From that day, she never touched her instrument again.

It is surprising that so many people have been so honest, for adults more commonly deny the importance of the things they weren't lucky enough to have or, alternatively, state that something potentially unpleasant that did happen had no lasting ill-effect. The conclusion has to be that the impact on children, young or older, of living either without apparent parental pleasure, acknowledgement or recognition, or with parents who push too hard for their own gain is clearly profound: it is a pattern that we should ensure does not get repeated.

91 Unblock your blocks to giving praise

Many people find it very hard to give praise. Some feel uncomfortable with using the unfamiliar words; some simply do not know what to praise while others squirm with disapproval at – or are deeply sceptical about – the whole process. The most common reasons people have to justify being sparing with praise include:
- that it can easily make a girl big-headed
- that praise should be given only for 'excellence': outstanding achievement and effort beyond expectation
- that if something could be better, it should not be praised as this could encourage laziness and send the wrong messages about general standards and expectations
- that a girl should be doing well in every sphere before she gets rewarded in case she takes a slide in an activity a parent thinks really matters
- that they created the success, not the girl, because they forced the study regime or paid for extra tuition, for example
- that previously it has had no impact, so they drop it

Some mothers may be slow to praise academic or other success if it rouses jealousy, makes them feel inferior or sharpens regret at missed opportunities.

Parents

* reflect on your childhood experiences and your current attitudes to giving and receiving praise. What has been your strongest influence?

* think hard to detect any difference in your treatment of girls and boys

* if you work outside the home, how do you praise people there, if at all? Do you have the same approach at home? If not, why not?

* give as you receive. When your daughter shows you affection and regard (both can be considered as praise) make sure you reciprocate

Teachers

* reflect on your past, at home and at school, and ponder on any patterns you could be repeating

* consider whether you find it easier to respond encouragingly in the classroom or at home with your own family, and think through why it might be so

92 Ask for it if you want to hear it

If you do not receive much positive feedback from family, work or friends, it is likely that you have learned to do without it. Men tend to be more self-sufficient, or like to consider themselves so, and may not even notice its absence. Women are more praise-hungry in childhood and are also more likely to miss getting pats on the back as adults.

If you want to hear it, ask for it; most 'significant others' are willing to be supportive once they realise that partners or friends want some back up. Very few will refuse you. Children can be encouraged to be appreciative after you have done something well, not just to be polite but as a genuine recognition of the special effort or achievement.

Those who think they can do without praise and consider it a big fuss about not very much will almost certainly find it harder to offer it to others. They may also think that for boys, especially, praise is unnecessary and girls should learn to grow up less needy of other people's approval. The best way to encourage a reluctant partner to become freer with his or her appreciation towards your daughter is to take a back route and praise and appreciate them overtly first.

Parents

* be specific. Analyse what you'd like to have more of, for example appreciation of your efforts or talents or acceptance of your views and values, then go and ask for it

* children tend to take what is done for them, at any level, as 'normal parenting'. It's hard for them to see that less might be done for them, so don't be harsh about their apparent insensitivity

* it is healthier to do something because you want to (in which case perhaps you don't need big thanks) rather than to curry favour. But if you'd like your efforts appreciated, describe that bit extra that you gave. Genuine thanks grow from genuine giving

Teachers

* think which job you consider you do well and whose appreciation you would value. Then go and seek confirmation and reinforcement

* positive feedback can come from colleagues, students and parents. How might each of these show their appreciation? What might you be entitled to expect?

93 If you did something well, believe it

In a world that seems obsessed with excellence, especially achievements that deliver big financial rewards, it can be hard to feel any pride in less obvious successes – or to realise that is what they are, given their modest scale.

People at work are increasingly being encouraged to identify and acknowledge their strengths and achievements. These might be relatively minor, such as responding sensitively to a junior member of staff who came in with a problem but left with a lighter step and a plan of action. In the home environment, there's no boss to offer compliments on your efforts that day, no daily target to meet. But we have good moments and successes nonetheless, and there are hundreds of tasks to be done, with or without our children, that involve the same efficiency skills, conflict resolution, stress management, practical, communication and listening skills that we have to demonstrate in the workplace.

Looking at what we did, and did well, rather than at what we did not do, will act as a boost and help us to be positive and encouraging with our daughters and partners.

Parents

* an appreciative child is one that smiles, is happy and shows affection to you. And sometimes she actually says thanks

* if you feel uncomfortable receiving praise, learn simply to say 'thank you' and hold onto it, don't bat it back

Teachers

* if you receive good feedback from a colleague, parent or student about something you have done, accept that it is valid. Don't squirm and claim you did not deserve it or the affirmation was uncalled for because it was just in the line of duty

94 Reward yourself

If you consider you have done something impressive, either given your starting point or because it represented a significant step towards a longer-term goal, reward yourself. Whatever is your special treat, allow yourself to have or do it.

It can be a private reward that you keep to yourself, or it could be something you choose to share with one other person. It might be sitting down with an easy-to-read trashy book, watching a film or DVD during the day, taking a long, scented bath, a drink with a friend or watching sports on TV all day one weekend.

Marking an achievement with a reward helps you to acknowledge that you got there, so you are entitled to take a break; it proves that you are not compelled always to go that one step further before you allow yourself to feel pleased; and it enables you to understand how your children might also value each small gesture of appreciation and feel their effort was worthwhile.

Parents

* think of things you might enjoy doing in any spare time, such as taking a walk or spending time in the garden. Remember these when you feel you deserve a small, or larger, treat

* the best reward is your own satisfaction; then there are no ifs and buts floating around in your head. Practise saying to yourself, 'That was well done! I can be really pleased about that'

* rewards don't always have to benefit you. You can share a treat or treat someone else if that gives you pleasure

Teachers

* reflect on the times during an inevitably pressured day that you might enjoy some respite when you feel you deserve it

* remember good enough success. Making a special effort, even if things didn't go entirely as planned, is worth marking otherwise you might not try again!

95 Accept any praise given to you

If someone praises you, accept it and hold onto it. Don't squirm with discomfort or hand it back as soon as you can with the words, 'It was nothing very special', 'I'm not sure what I've done to deserve a comment like that' or 'I was going to do it anyway'. Girls and women are particularly prone to such self-denigration. They may have tried hard but they usually believe that they should have done that anyway, which makes the effort seem commonplace, not worthy of comment.

If you often feel you don't deserve any recognition or accolade and you instead feel embarrassed when someone tells you you have done well, you may imagine others feel the same, including your child. This makes it more likely you will be sparing with your praise, to protect her from the expected discomfort.

But this reticence is not helpful. Far better to change your mindset and learn to accept positive feedback with good grace when you are fortunate enough to receive it!

Parents

* practise saying 'thank you' when you are given praise, and teach your daughters to do the same

* don't make a joke about giving or hearing praise until everyone in the family knows that, mostly, it is given straight and can be trusted. Only then is it safe to lighten things with a bit of fun, and then only on the odd occasion

Teachers

* if any student says, 'that was good fun!' or 'that was interesting', respond with a thank you rather than 'good'. Her comment is intended as complimentary feedback, not to make you realise she enjoyed it

96 Don't compete against your daughter

My mother was so competitive with all of us daughters. She always had to claim that she knew more than us, could do things faster than us, had read this book or that one by the time she was our age, had travelled as much and, later, that her marriage to our father was more successful than ours with our husbands. It was so sad and probably meant she felt very insecure, but during my childhood it made me feel she could never be proud of me. It also made it hard to be proud of myself.

Avoid competing against your daughter. Some mothers and fathers find it hard to give their children the space to become better than, more beautiful than, more skilled than themselves. But growing girls need to feel respected for their achievements, not constantly pushed into a parent's shade.

Parents

* becoming competitive is more likely to switch her off than spur her to greater effort as it could make her feel overpowered and dejected

* if you are competitive with her, she's more likely to be so with others

* avoid referring to your past to claim any superior edge because you will almost certainly not have remembered the time or event accurately

Teachers

* 'clever clogs' students may become irritating but never try to trip them up with difficult questions or be tempted to beat them in a competitive exchange of knowledge

97 Show respect for the other parent

It is not always possible for both biological parents to live together under the same roof. However, despite the actual living arrangements, it will help any girl to work and grow healthily and happily if each parent is not only involved to some degree in her schooling and upbringing but also is shown a measure of regard by the other one. If a father fails to compliment her mother or shows actual disrespect, a girl could find herself torn between them; she may doubt herself as a growing female or find it hard to trust males.

If her mother speaks only ill of her father, this will raise questions about how much of him lives on in her, creating aspects of herself that she may find uncomfortable.

Parents

* parents need to earn the respect of their daughter as she matures and becomes more discriminating. She will gauge how well they treat each other and others, and judge whether either deserves her respect

* watch your words and reactions as you watch films or television together. Swearing, making catcalls or other derogatory remarks often imply disrespect

* fathers or father figures are important to girls, especially when they enter puberty, so fathers should offer plenty of love and positive feedback. Brothers, uncles or cousins could offer alternative affirmation

Teachers

* every school should adopt sexual harassment and anti-discrimination policies. Girls and female staff should, of course, treat their male colleagues and peers with the same respect

* gender awareness and equality of regard should apply throughout the school and in every lesson to help boys and girls flourish equally

98 Enjoy your own company and that of others

The best thing about having friends is you can assume they spend time with you because they enjoy your company. If they didn't, they wouldn't. They let you know that you are good to be around, which at times can be quite intoxicating – and of course they are also there to share your problems if you ever need them as well as providing a great source of fun.

Enjoying the company of your friends will help you to realise why it is good to enjoy the company of your daughter. It will make her feel valued and appreciate that she is someone who is able to give other people pleasure rather than be a source of disappointment and strife and will provide an enormous boost to her confidence. If you give time to your friends but also show you value and enjoy your daughter because you preserve time for her, she will get the true measure of her value to you. Having and enjoying your friends therefore offers a double benefit, provided they don't crowd her out.

Parents

* 'I've had a lovely day with my friends, and now I'm having a lovely time with you. Aren't I lucky?'

* if you take your daughter with you when you meet friends, make sure she feels involved either in the group or with something you take for her to do

* be careful if you collect your younger children from school that they don't feel ignored as they emerge because you are deep in conversation with others. Greet them warmly each time

* enjoyment is a product of engaging with the present, the here and now

Teachers

* enjoy your students by talking to them as you see them around the building between lessons

* take time to enjoy yourself with colleagues in the staff room rather than working continuously

99 Endorse yourself

Children reap dividends when parents are comfortable with themselves. This entails accepting personal histories and the decisions that have been made, or not made, in earlier years. We should not continue to beat ourselves up for anything that happened or put the shutters down on the past and pretend that certain events did not happen. The more content we feel with ourselves, the less we will be tempted to relive or deny things through our children and the more we will be able to support and encourage them in healthy ways that reflect and give space to their true selves.

If we think we are not valuable or nothing we do is ever good enough, it is tempting to fill the emptiness that we feel inside with our daughter's successes or failures, and too easy to fashion an identity based on those, and to mould her to suit. We are likely to be more demanding of success and more grudging in giving praise, waiting until we feel it is really deserved. If she makes a mistake, we could feel it as a reflection on us, so we may either undermine the importance of the event or criticise her to protect our self-image.

Parents

* write down your strong points

* identify your regrets. But every cloud has a silver lining; nothing is ever a total disaster. For every decision or event you regret in the past, try to identify a positive personal trait or outcome that arose from it

* think of everything you have done to help others. Achievement is not just scored by publicly accepted measures

Teachers

* write down your professional strengths and enjoy and cherish these attributes

* list your weaker traits and consider how much they genuinely set you back

* consider how much you pressure your students to cover up your feared weaknesses

* try to accept that school should help students to thrive academically and socially and to mature in many ways. Recall instances when you have helped a student to grow and develop, not just pass the exams

100 Encourage yourself

Good parenting is not about perfection because it is impossible to get it absolutely right all the time. In any case, people differ in their views about what is the right, or best, response for any situation, so it is not a practical goal. We make mistakes as parents – lots of them – just as growing girls do. We need encouraging pats on the back for doing our best: for trying new and more positive ways to say things to our daughters; for trying to understand more about how they think and learn and about parent-child relationship dynamics – just as girls need encouragement. Our intentions and efforts are important; and these will often be enough to bring about noticeable changes in attitude and performance that need to be recognised in order to encourage further self-enhancing changes.

The future must look enticing. We are doing well enough and we can make changes to make the future look rosier. Our girls can and will do well and we should help them to imagine and expect a positive future by creating an atmosphere of hope, belief and appreciation for everyone in the family, in the here and now.

Parents

* setbacks are normal – part of the ebb and flow of life. The future will be bright, and we will feel more encouraged if we apply some of the tips offered within these pages

* don't beat yourself up: apply the recommended 4:1 praise to criticism / blame ratio to yourself. Each time you think you fall short, find four things to do or that you have already done that you can feel pleased about

* 'true power does not reveal itself' (Foucault, French philosopher). Providing a home in which each individual is empowered and able to explore their potential, quirks and interests without pressure and intrusive guidance is the healthy way forward

Teachers

* teaching is part of your life but not all of it. Think of all the other ways to accept and evaluate yourself – community or church activist, parent, partner, son or daughter – and be positive about your overall contribution

* be encouraged – the future is almost always rich and rosy if you open yourself to opportunities, and think positive!

Postscript

In case you have reached the end of the book and feel a little swamped and confused by the 'oughts' and 'buts' having read it straight through, here are some suggestions and summaries.

Taking a broad view, far more children suffer today from not being praised enough than are being damaged by excessive or misplaced praise. Children have a profound need not only to be noticed by the close adults in their life but also to be affirmed, appreciated and enjoyed. Spending time with children can be difficult when everyone is so pressured, but all efforts to do so will be amply rewarded with warmth and love from a child who feels secure and self-confident and wants, and knows how, to have fun as well as to do well.

It is said that we remember a maximum of ten per cent of what we hear or read at any one time. Having been faced with 100 tips and many more bullets, it might help to sift through your thoughts by writing down ten things that have remained clear and on which you could take action confidently. Perhaps some of these could be placed in the 'good things to do' side and some on the 'best avoided' side. Prioritise these, try them out over a few days and then dip into the book again to expand your repertoire from these experiences. Some will work for you, some may not. The important guidance is to use what strategies you feel comfortable with, provided they seem to have a positive impact on your daughter.